"Those of us who carry the legacy of the Holocaust understand why and how the story isn't over. In fact, for many of us the search has just begun. There are questions and memories that have not only been too terrifying to face, but also some have even been considered forbidden. How do we face or even dare to reveal the agony of abuse from a parent? Their rage would remain a deep secret, a terrible source of shame. In her book, *"From Generation to Generation: Healing Intergenerational Trauma Through Storytelling*," Emily Wanderer Cohen defies the boundaries of fear and, with a tremendous sense of courage, opens up a safe space for dialogue. We are known as "The People of the Book." We are taught that through words we became part of creation. May these words be part of the healing one generation most definitely prayed to bestow upon the next and the next."

- CHAYA ROSEN, author of *"In the Shadow of God, Poems of Memory and Healing"*

"Emily Wanderer Cohen makes an invaluable contribution to our understanding of how historical trauma is inherited and how it manifests in our daily lives. With courage, insight and compassion for her mother, and the traumatized generation who survived the Holocaust,

Emily breaks an unspoken taboo and unflinchingly bears witness to her own suffering as a Second Generation survivor. Out of the specificity of her transformative story emerge universal truths that can guide us on our own healing journeys. At once a memoir, as well as a workbook for descendants of any historical trauma wanting to transform their own wounding, Emily's moving narrative demonstrates the power of self-revelatory storytelling to unburden and heal a traumatic past."

- ARMAND VOLKAS, MFT, RDT/BCT, Psychotherapist, Drama Therapist and Theatre Director, son of resistance fighters and Auschwitz survivors, Director of Healing the Wounds of History Institute

"Emily Wanderer Cohen has written a book with such BRUTAL HONESTY, that I actually—physically—found myself shaking while reading it. Her writing is revelatory, BLUNT, and poetic in its NONCONFORMITY. As a fellow Holocaust artist and historian, I say with complete conviction that this book will be a voice for our entire generation in ways that NOTHING before it has. An EXTRAORDINARY work of art... a MUST read."

- TOBY GOTESMAN SCHNEIER, Holocaust artist and historian

"Emily Wanderer Cohen has written a powerful and poignant memoir about what it means to grow up as the child of a Holocaust survivor. *From Generation to Generation* doesn't pull any punches—it exposes ongoing consequences of the atrocities of the Holocaust of which most of us are totally unaware. While important for the second and third generation survivors, this book is even more relevant for the rest of us. The horrors of the Holocaust don't die with the survivors. Cohen's book reminds us that 70+ years later, there's still work to do."

- LINDA POPKY, author of "*Marketing Above the Noise: Achieve Strategic Advantage with Marketing that Matters*"

From Generation to Generation

FROM
GENERATION
_to_ GENERATION

Healing Intergenerational Trauma
Through Storytelling

EMILY WANDERER COHEN

NEW YORK

LONDON • NASHVILLE • MELBOURNE • VANCOUVER

From Generation to Generation

Healing Intergenerational Trauma Through Storytelling

© 2018 Emily Wanderer Cohen

Published in New York, New York, by Morgan James Publishing in partnership with Difference Press. Morgan James is a trademark of Morgan James, LLC. www.MorganJamesPublishing.com

The Morgan James Speakers Group can bring authors to your live event. For more information or to book an event visit The Morgan James Speakers Group at www.TheMorganJamesSpeakersGroup.com.

ISBN 9781683507574 paperback
ISBN 9781683507581 eBook
Library of Congress Control Number: 2017913989

Cover Design by:
Rachel Lopez
www.r2cdesign.com

Interior Design by:
Chris Treccani
www.3dogcreative.net

In an effort to support local communities, raise awareness and funds, Morgan James Publishing donates a percentage of all book sales for the life of each book to Habitat for Humanity Peninsula and Greater Williamsburg.

Get involved today! Visit
www.MorganJamesBuilds.com

For Josh and Rachael, who witnessed Mutti traumatize me even as an adult. The cycle stops with you. I love you both.

And for Mutti, I forgive you.

There is no greater agony than bearing an untold story inside you.

– Maya Angelou

CONTENTS

INTRODUCTION

I didn't start to write this book. Rather, I started writing what most second-generation Holocaust survivors (2Gs) write: their Holocaust survivor parent's story. I felt driven to document it even though Mutti (mother in German and what I called my mom) had completed a video interview for the USC Shoah Foundation and had given many talks about her experiences—some of which were on videotape, too—to middle- and high-school students in Portland and Seattle. I wanted to get it "on paper" once and for all.

But when I handed over my first essay to my neighbor, a former high-school English teacher and writing coach who had graciously offered to help me write some essays that might or might not eventually turn into a book, she said, "Emily, where are you in this story?" I replied, "It's not my story, it's Mutti's story." She looked at me in complete disbelief. "Is it?" she asked me.

For the next week or so, I kept thinking about her words. Was she right? Was it actually MY story that needed to be told? Slowly, I began to put myself into the essays, but getting in touch with my emotions—beyond the overriding anger and resentment I felt—was extremely difficult. Each week, thinking I had dug as deeply as possible, my neighbor would push me to go deeper.

I started to feel exposed, naked, all my imperfections on display for the reader to see. Then I realized something: I had such a difficult time getting in touch with those feelings because I had put them out of my mind in order to survive the years of emotional and physical abuse. I couldn't feel sadness, shame, and hurt because I had taught myself NOT to feel those emotions, focusing instead on anger and resentment.

Which was exactly what Mutti had to do in concentration camp: ignore her emotions in order to survive. By focusing her anger and resentment toward Hitler and the Nazis—even long after the Holocaust ended—she was able to continue living. Every day was a struggle for her, I realize this now. I spent so much time being angry with Mutti for her inability to let go of her anger, and being resentful of her for abusing me, that I couldn't feel compassion for her. The clear perpetuation of Holocaust trauma was too obvious to ignore. And that is how this book came to be.

I realize that not every 2G experienced exactly what I did and I would never imply that "one size fits all" with respect to transferred Holocaust trauma. In my discussions with other 2Gs, and some 3Gs, there are some definite similarities (e.g., many of us felt the omnipresence of the Holocaust in our houses and the sense that nothing we ever experienced could ever match the horror our parents lived through)—as well as some striking differences.

Of course, how each of us reacted to our parents' trauma varied widely, too. Every 2G's experience is different—just as every Holocaust survivor's experience was different. What's important is that we not judge each other by saying, "I didn't experience that," but that we understand the origin of the trauma and support each other in healing ourselves and breaking the cycle with future generations. And one very powerful way to break that cycle is through writing.

It's well known that writing can be a significant factor in healing from trauma. Many books have been published, most famously by Dr. James Pennebaker and Louise DeSalvo, about how writing can improve emotional health and ease the pain of trauma experiences. And that is exactly what happened to me as I started to write my story.

While writing, I started to feel lighter, happier, more centered, and a feeling of forgiveness toward my Mutti—which I had never encountered before—came over me. They say that there is a "hidden price of silence," which is grounded in scientific research, and I certainly felt that before I started writing. Anger, resentment, depression, and anxiety—all of these feelings were common for me. Writing has released the pressure and helped me heal from the trauma Mutti had been transmitting to me for 50 years. I now have a new, positive outlook on life. I can't wait to wake up and see what each day has in store.

The more I wrote, the more I could see connections between Mutti's trauma and my upbringing—and my behaviors and decisions as an adult. I had been traumatized every day by the Holocaust; I couldn't get away from it. The trauma transmitted to me by Mutti. I've explored some of the connections in this book, but there are certainly more yet to be discovered. As scientific research continues to present evidence that trauma is indeed passed down genetically, my curiosity and desire to delve deeper into these stories keeps growing.

Through writing, I discovered direct relationships that I hadn't seen before even though they were literally right under my nose. Sometimes, I began a chapter as an exploration, thinking it would end a certain way and it took a completely different turn halfway through writing—and resulted in a significant "a-ha" moment. Other times, I knew exactly what the connection was between Mutti's experiences and my triggers before I started. Either way, the act of writing about these connections solidified in my mind how powerful writing can be in healing from second-hand trauma. And because of this, I have been helping others do the same, and many of my clients have told me that they have felt the grip of trauma release as they write.

Neither I nor other 2Gs can just "get over" our experiences; it's in our genes. The transferred trauma can manifest itself as PTSD (post-traumatic stress disorder), violence, substance abuse, risky behavior, and self-harm. It's not pretty, but it's our reality.

I kept all of these experiences inside me for so long and only discovered true inner peace and forgiveness through storytelling. My sincere hope is that, as you read my stories and nod through some of them, you realize that you are not alone in your transmitted trauma and that you decide to write your way to healing and forgiveness as well.

At the end of each chapter, I have included writing prompts to spur your memories, creativity, and ultimately, your transmitted trauma story. These prompts relate to the general theme of the chapter, but you may have other topics or themes you want to explore, and I encourage you to do that. Remember, no two 2G, 3G, or 4G stories are the same.

Writing about painful memories can be tremendously healing when you are able to look at the events and your feelings objectively, as words on a piece of paper rather than unresolved, unspoken emotions held deep inside. Writing can also feel safer than speaking with a family member or therapist, because no one is interrupting your train of thought, disagreeing with the sequence of events, or questioning your motives or emotions.

In my work with other 2Gs—as well as 3Gs and 4Gs—Holocaust survivors on documenting their stories, I have seen some incredible results. One client told me, in our initial discovery session, that he constantly felt his mother over his shoulder, still judging and berating him, even though she had passed away several years ago. He lived with this weight each and every day. A Hollywood producer, he was always nervous, would second-guess himself, and he was visibly upset when we talked about his life. After working with me to write his story, he has become calmer, more confident, and has been able to look forward rather than backward at the past. He tells me that writing about his transmitted Holocaust trauma has changed his life for the better: he no longer hears his mother's judgmental voice on every decision he makes. He feels free. He's happier than he's ever been.

Another client told me that she was concerned that talking about her grandfather's Holocaust history—and how it affected her—would make her a target for anti-Semitism, so she kept it a secret. Unfortunately, doing so only caused her greater pain and suffering—and kept her children and grandchildren suffering as well: They had no idea how the Holocaust affected their family and, most importantly, why their mother and grandmother were so resistant to talk about their feelings. She was completely shut down emotionally. When she called me, she was desperate: Her daughter had just given birth to yet another grandchild and she was sensing a strong desire to expose the family secrets, but she was still worried. We worked together to write her family's story as well as her feelings about it, so that her children and grandchildren would understand how difficult it was for her to tell the stories—and explain her fears so they would abide by her wishes. Since then, she has realized that worrying about anti-Semites and other outsiders is less important than communicating her family's history to her progeny, and she now freely discusses both the facts and her emotions with her children and grandchildren. She is planning a trip to Poland to explore her family's roots, which she never considered before.

Through this book, I hope that you—the children, grandchildren, and great-grandchildren of Holocaust survivors—can see how storytelling can help you heal from the transmitted trauma of the Holocaust and stop suffering in silence. I hope you can embrace the themes of each chapter—and find more themes of your own—so you can forge a new path and approach life from a new perspective. The journey of letting go is full of surprises and can be incredibly liberating. And it can help you uncover the greatness of who you are meant to be.

CHAPTER ONE

The Fly Swatter

It's seven o'clock in the morning and I'm getting ready for school. The school bus will be here in 20 minutes and I am still trying to cover the bald spot on the left side of my head. I add more gel and brush again. Nope, still not right. Even more gel. Another few brushstrokes. Sigh, it still looks so obvious. Mutti walks into the bathroom, without knocking on the closed door, and reaches out to help me. I flinch and sputter, "Please leave me alone" through my tears. Mutti stomps back out of the bathroom, but not before she says, "You know you deserved that, don't you?"

As far back as I can remember, Mutti's weapon of choice for punishment was the fly swatter. It hung on the wall in the kitchen next to the refrigerator. Sea green plastic head, gray handle. Whenever I misbehaved or talked back to Mutti, she would make a beeline to the kitchen, take the fly swatter off the wall, and run back to wherever I was, waving the fly swatter in the air as if warning what was to come.

And when I saw her running with the swatter, I would try to hide, sometimes only making it as far as the corner of my bed, sometimes crawling under my bed, and other times making it into the closet with louvered doors in my room with time to spare. Either way, Mutti always found me and hit me over and over, while I cowered and tried to lessen the impact of the swatter with my hands. Sometimes, I would seek refuge in the bathroom, which had a lock, but even that didn't stop Mutti. She'd pick the lock with her fingernail and come after me while I sat in the bathtub, curled in a ball.

No amount of crying or begging on my part would make Mutti stop the hitting. At some point she would get tired, I guess, and stop. Then, she would simply walk away, while I continued to whimper or cry in pain, still shaking.

Often, I didn't even know what I had done to anger Mutti. We would be having a conversation and it was like a switch would flip. She became enraged—yes, rage is the right word—and I knew what was coming. One of the telltale signs of impending rage was the look in Mutti's eyes: When Mutti got angry, her eyes would change from their usual green to a steely gray, or at least it seemed that way to me. But more than just changing color, her eyes would become vacant and unexpressive, as if no one was really there. She wouldn't listen to me either, as if she couldn't hear me. Reflecting back on those times, I think Mutti left the present and went back to Germany in her mind, to the concentration camps and the terror she experienced in them.

Research has shown that victims often become per-petrators—and that certainly was the case for me. I felt that I was being punished for the horrible things that happened to Mutti before I was even born. Because she could not fight back when the Nazis came to pick her up or when they beat her in camp, I was the surrogate. I was the SS officer who made her dig graves in the Polish snow. I was the guard who ordered her to sew buttons onto Nazi uniforms faster, even as she sewed one on and then cut it off discreetly to slow down her output. She was passing her trauma down to me, one 'thwap' of the fly swatter at a time.

I spent a lot of my childhood with a knot in my stomach, never knowing when Mutti would snap. I walked on eggshells. Like most children, I just wanted to be loved and told I was 'good enough'. But that wasn't Mutti. I can't even remember being held, snuggled with, or soothed as a child. What I do remember is that I desperately wanted her to say something—anything—positive. And the more desperate I became for her attention and acceptance, the more emotionally distant and unavailable she became.

When Mutti was really angry, she added pulling on—and out—my hair to the fly swatter treatment. After she was done chasing me around the house with the fly swatter, she would grab a clump of hair and yank as hard as she could. I remember staring at her fist, my dark brown hair poking out of both sides like a clump of long grass. Do you know how long it takes for a clump of hair to grow back?

Going to school the day after a swatter episode was an exercise in covering the welts and hiding my shame. Most of the time, my arms took the brunt of the punishment, so I wore a long-sleeved sweater to hide the marks.

Sometimes, when the swatter met my neck, I needed a turtleneck sweater. And when Mutti decided to scratch and claw at me, sometimes scratching my face, I had to use make-up to cover the marks.

Mutti's outbursts of anger and physical abuse didn't stop when I was an adult, but they were less frequent since she lived in Seattle and I lived in the Bay Area. Two incidents stand out in my mind.

The first was when my daughter was 15 months old. Mutti was visiting from Seattle and we were going as a family to the Nutcracker Ballet in San Francisco. It was a Sunday morning, and my daughter needed a bath before we went to the ballet. I put her in the bathtub and asked Mutti to watch her while I made tea. When I came back to check on them, my daughter was alone in the bathroom, still in the tub. I called Mutti a couple of times and, eventually, she came walking back into the bathroom as if nothing had happened. When I asked why she left my daughter alone, Mutti got angry and defensive. I saw Mutti's eyes change color and recognized the vacant stare. Then she reached out, grabbed my finger, and twisted it.

My finger hurt, but I didn't think it was broken. We went to the ballet anyway, barely speaking to each other.

By the end of the performance, my finger had swelled up so much that I decided to go to the ER. The doctor took an X-ray and said I had a spiral fracture. He asked how I had done that, and I lied. I don't remember exactly what I told the doctor about how it happened, but I do remember that the same feeling of shame I felt as a child when Mutti hit me washed over my entire body. And I lied to my friends about the injury afterward as well. Whose mother does that, especially when they are 30-something years old?

The next time I saw Mutti's eyes go vacant was the day I took away her car keys forever.

"Mutti, stay in bed until I get back from the store with your medications," I sternly advised while tucking her in her bed, her walker in the living room to dissuade her from attempting to get up. I had just brought her home from rehab, where she had spent the last two weeks after a knee replacement.

When I returned to her apartment an hour later, the smell of something burning overpowered me. I looked into the kitchen, to my right, and I saw the source: a pot on the stove, burner on high, but nothing in the pot. The bottom of the pot was black. I turned off the burner and grabbed the handle of the pot to move it to the sink.

"Slam!"

Without a potholder, the pot handle was too hot and I dropped it. The heat from the pot scorched Mutti's white linoleum floor, melting a square.

"Damn it!" I screamed. "Mutti!!!!! Mutti????" No answer.

As I approached the bathroom, I could hear Mutti whistling quietly. I stood at the doorway and found her puttering around, rearranging toiletries, completely oblivious to the burning smell or me standing in front of her. She didn't have her hearing aid in.

"Mutti, I told you not to get out of bed!" I yelled.

"So? I did. Big deal," she snapped.

"Aside from the fact that you could have fallen and hurt yourself, you also could have burned down the building! Don't you smell the burning?" I was livid and my voice was shaking.

"Ach, Em, you're always overreacting. Don't tell me what to do! I am your mother!" she said defensively as she pushed past me to go to her bedroom. I saw her go straight for her purse—and her car keys.

"You're not going anywhere, especially not in your car!" I screamed.

I grabbed Mutti's keys out of her hand.

At that moment, her eyes changed once again. She grabbed my hand and tried to get back her keys. She didn't connect with the keys, but she managed to take hold of my favorite bracelet. Interestingly, the bracelet was one made of Turkish evil eyes, which are said to protect the wearer from evil and harm. Mutti pulled hard. The bracelet broke. I cried, not only for the loss of the bracelet, but also for the loss of the mother I never really had.

YOUR TURN:

- What was punishment like in your house?
- If you had siblings, was punishment the same for all of you or were different siblings punished differently?
- Do you remember how you felt while you were being punished? What emotions did you feel?
- Were you able to sense, in advance, when your parent/grandparent might get angry? Was there a sign? Was it predictable or unpredictable?
- If you were never punished physically, why do you think that was the case?
- Can you connect the way your parent/grandparent punished you to their Holocaust story in some way?

CHAPTER TWO

E is for Emily

Here it comes again: the all-too-familiar sense of panic when I misplace or lose something. This time, it's my silver Cal pin that I love dearly. I thought I put it in my jewelry box after the game last weekend, but it's not there. I can't rest until I find it. I sob while I search frantically. I shake and tremble at the thought of losing my pin. I cancel plans so I can keep searching for it. And I start deriding myself: Why am I so stupid? Why do I always lose things? I should be more careful with valuables. I'm so irresponsible. Mutti was right, I *am* an idiot.

This scene has played out many times throughout my life, with items as valuable as my wedding ring to things as insignificant as a pair of nail scissors. I simply cannot accept that I am human, humans lose things, humans make mistakes, humans are not perfect. And I can't shake the sound of Mutti's voice in my head. I still expect to be punished for losing something. Mutti is no longer here to punish me, so I punish myself, continuing to inflict trauma on myself.

As far back as I can remember, Mutti wore a gold belt-buckle ring on her right hand, the band split from wear. It was the only possession Mutti managed to save from Nazi confiscation; everything else was lost or taken away. Whenever an officer approached her and asked her to give him the ring, the story went, she would turn it over, show the split in the band and say, "You don't want this. It's broken." That ring, although fairly simple and small, was more valuable than anything else in the world to Mutti.

It was also the item I resented the most in my childhood, because whenever I lost or misplaced something, Mutti would talk about how she never lost or misplaced that ring—or anything else. She was perfect, she didn't make mistakes. I, on the other hand, was imperfect and made mistakes all the time. And my imperfections and mistakes were met with punishment rather than empathy and compassion. I was petrified of admitting any imperfection or loss.

One day stands out more than any other. In fact, I still go over the events of that day to see if I missed something, if there was something I could have done to prevent the result. If a genie magically appeared and let me have a do-over for one day, this day would be it.

It was a hot and sunny July afternoon in Portland and the Somerset West pool was packed with kids. I had ridden my yellow bike with the coveted banana seat and white basket with plastic flowers mounted in front of the handlebars to the pool. I was meeting some friends and I remember being gloriously happy at the prospect of spending several hours diving in the deep end and trying to reach the bottom before running out of breath.

When I opened the door to the pool clubhouse, I was greeted by the smell of chlorine and a slippery, wet cement floor. Behind the check-in desk, clean white towels waiting for eager swimmers were piled on one side; mounds of wet, stinky ones on the other. Nearby, stacks of ubiquitous green mesh hanging baskets, the ones with pockets in which to put your clothes and other belongings while you swam.

I checked in with the teenager working the front desk that day, grabbed a towel and a green mesh basket, and walked into the women's locker room. I found a changing stall and hung up the green bag, rushing to take off my sandals, t-shirt, and shorts and put on my swimsuit to meet my friends, who were already there.

After swimming and diving into the deep end for a few hours, we were all exhausted and decided to go to my house for something to eat. Still dripping and with a towel around me, I walked back to the locker room and took a shower. I went to the changing stall where I had left the green mesh bag and got dressed. I put my hand in the pocket of my shorts to retrieve my round, gold signet ring that my parents had given me for my 12th birthday.

The ring wasn't there. I was now panicking uncontrollably, hyperventilating. Where is my ring?

I searched the cement floor around me. Under the bench. In the next stall. In the showers. I enlisted my friends' help, but after about 30 minutes of searching, it was clear: my ring was gone. Stolen. I was heartbroken. But I also knew what awaited me at home.

I rode my bike home, still sobbing. I snuck past Mutti in the kitchen, went straight to my room and shut the door. But Mutti's sixth sense was working overtime that day. She barged into my room without regard for the closed door (which wasn't entirely unprecedented; Mutti didn't respect any boundaries) and said, "Ok, Em, what's wrong?"

"Nothing," I replied, but somehow she knew. My heart beat wildly as I watched her gaze fall to my hand.

"Where's your ring?" she asked.

"Mutti, I don't know what happened. I put my ring in my shorts pocket so no one would see it but someone stole it," I said between sobs.

"Ach, Em! How could you be so careless and irresponsible?" Mutti yelled. "Why did you have it at the pool anyway? You should have left it at home."

"But Mutti, it wasn't my fault. Someone STOLE it," I protested.

"I don't care," Mutti said. "Well, don't you dare think we'll replace it. You don't deserve nice things. You clearly can't take care of them."

I remember crying in my room for hours. The last thing I wanted or needed was Mutti's criticism and scorn. I had lost something that meant a lot to me, and I felt bad enough. And even though I had known it was coming before I returned home, I couldn't protect myself from the pain and hurt of Mutti's reaction.

Mutti's verbal abuse was not limited to times when I lost something, however. If I made a mistake or demonstrated any imperfection, I was punished as well, and she would often hold herself up as an example of what I should try to achieve. She never admitted making a mistake, never admitted fault, and certainly never, ever said she was sorry. Apologizing was a foreign concept to Mutti.

Clearly, the Holocaust and her time in concentration camp molded this behavior. Admitting a mistake or even making one in full view could mean the difference between life and death. Prisoners had to be perfect or at least not do anything to draw the attention of the Nazi guards or officers. The Holocaust taught Mutti that she could not admit or take blame for anything. And she transmitted that trauma to me.

I remember coming home from middle school with an A- on my report card, one A- amid five other As. I was pretty proud of that report card, but when Mutti saw it she zeroed in on that A- and said, "Well, why isn't that an A too?" The message was clear: The only way to survive in life was to be perfect, and being perfect in school would pave the way for success. Schoolwork and good grades were more important than anything else was in our house, and only activities that Mutti approved of were allowed, e.g., playing violin, orchestra, ballet, and ice skating. My pleas to join the swim team or play soccer were ignored. Not only would she not drive me, I was forbidden from asking anyone else for a ride. It was a flat-out no.

I must admit that not responding the same way to my children's grades or mistakes as Mutti reacted to mine is extremely difficult. I try to check myself, not wanting to transmit this trauma to my kids, but I'm not always successful. When I'm impatient with them or disappointed in a grade or other outcome and express my disappointment, I feel horrible. I know that I am repeating how Mutti treated me and I hate myself for it. I try to close my eyes and take a few deep breaths, reminding myself that I don't want to continue the cycle. Have you ever noticed yourself passing the same judgment and criticism of your parent onto your child or grandchild?

My fear of making a mistake and the derision I would receive from Mutti for making one continues to be a theme in my life today. When faced with a decision, I can be paralyzed into complete indecision, fearing that the choice I make will be the wrong one—and it won't be correctable.

Truth be told, it's a two-fold fear: first, of making a mistake in the first place and second, of being unable to correct course or change the decision. I have tossed and turned all night with worry many times. "What if that's the wrong choice? What if I can't fix it?" goes through my head.

Today, most people subscribe to the theory that making mistakes is an important part of the learning process, especially for children, and that you learn as much—or more—from failure as you can from success. It takes every ounce of my willpower to remind myself of that, both in my own endeavors and pursuits and those of my children. Not because I want to coddle or protect my kids from failure or disappointment, but because the need (not simple desire) to be perfect has been so strongly ingrained in me. Another legacy of the Holocaust.

Given all of this, it was more than a little ironic when the Rabbi approached me as I was walking with my family from the small cemetery chapel to Mutti's grave at Neveh Zedek Cemetery on December 24th, 2014.

"Emily, we have a little problem. When the gravediggers started digging on the left side of the plot, where your mother was supposed to be buried, according to the existing headstone, their spades immediately hit a pine coffin," the Rabbi said.

"Oh my G-d, for 30 years I've been putting the stone on the WRONG side of the grave?! On an empty grave? Vati (father in German and what I called my dad) was on the OTHER side?" I thought, but didn't say out loud.

"Given what you told me about your mom's perfectionism, I don't understand how this happened," continued the Rabbi.

Neither did I, and I became somewhat obsessed with how it happened. Did the cemetery bury him on the wrong side? Did the granite company engrave the headstone incorrectly? And along with that obsession, I felt that I had to make it "right." I had to "fix" it. Because that's what Mutti would want. Because of HER perfectionism and hatred of mistakes.

I continued my obsession with making it right—which meant erasing the entire headstone and re-engraving Mutti's and Vati's names on the correct sides, corresponding to where their bodies were actually buried—for four months. For that entire time, I felt sure that the error had been on the cemetery's side or the memorial company's side. There was no way Mutti, with her crazy attention to detail and perfectionism, made this mistake.

However, when I finally sifted through Mutti's papers hoping to find the name of the granite company at which I could point a finger and make them foot the bill for the change, what I found was something else entirely: a sketch of the gravestone inscription for Vati, in Mutti's handwriting. The inscription was on the right-hand side. At this point, sitting on the grey Berber carpet in my office, with Mutti's papers spread in front of me, I realized there was no one to blame—but Mutti.

I was still obsessed with fixing it, making it perfect, until I found out the cost to do so was $1500 more than leaving it as-is. I began to think: For whom am I doing this? For me? For Mutti? For my kids?

When I asked my daughter what she thought, she said, "I think it's kind of funny. It can be our family secret." So, after six months of ruminating, I finally decided to leave it alone. Let it be a family secret. I'll always go to the cemetery and put the stone on the right for Vati and on the left for Mutti, chuckling the entire time.

Oh, and true to her word, Mutti never did replace the ring.

YOUR TURN:

- Did you feel intense pressure to be a high achiever in school and other activities?
- Did your parents have unreasonable expectations of you?
- Did your parents compare you to themselves in any way, making you feel inferior? Or were they overly attentive and loving?
- Have you found yourself passing down the trauma (pressure to not make mistakes, unreasonably high expectations) to your children?
- What role did items of value (e.g., jewelry, silverware, art, etc.) have in your household?
- Are there particular items of value that you feel anxiety or panic if you misplace or lose them?
- Can you draw any connections between your parent's/grandparent's Holocaust experience (concentration camp, labor camp, in hiding, escape, etc.) and their expectations of you?
- Did you discover any vulnerability your parent/grandparent was trying to hide?

CHAPTER THREE

You Can't Always Get What You Want

"Every day I walked by those red patent leather shoes in the window at Wertheim on the way to school," Mutti recalled. "And the more I asked for those shoes, the less chance I had of getting them."

This was the story I heard every time I asked Mutti for something, anything. It could have been as small as a cookie at the bakery or as large as my own car. The answer Mutti gave in response to my requests was always, always, "No."

While this was difficult and upsetting in my younger years, leading to temper tantrums on my part and the inevitable fly-swatter punishment by Mutti, it became completely untenable in my teenage years. All I wanted to do, like every teen, was fit in and have the "right" clothes, but Mutti made sure that was as difficult as possible. She even articulated her belief that because she couldn't have what she wanted when she was young—first because of my grandfather, Opi, and then because "Hitler took everything away"—I couldn't have what I wanted either.

Mutti did everything in her power to make me suffer and feel the pain of denial as she had. But, of course, I really had no leg to stand on because my "suffering" would never compare to her Holocaust experience. Deep down I knew that, I suppose, although that didn't stop me from declaring how unfair and unreasonable she was being. I was a typical teenager in that way.

Denying me material possessions that afforded me social status was just one form of punishment, taking away simple privileges was another. However, her revocation of privileges had far-reaching consequences for me, while the themes of my social acceptance and independence from Mutti continued to play a starring role.

I don't remember the series of events that led up to Mutti taking away the keys to the Chevy Chevette the first time, but I could not get to the Jewish Community Center (JCC) for my monthly B'nai Brith Girls (BBG), a Jewish youth group, meeting. While that may sound trivial, add in the fact that I had recently been elected president of my chapter, Theodor Herzl BBG #1393, and the ramifications of my lack of attendance increased greatly. Then multiply that by five times in a six-month period and the deal was sealed: I had to resign my position because my mother wouldn't let me get to the meetings. No one else in the chapter lived nearby, so getting a ride with another member wasn't an option.

When I first mentioned to Mutti that I was going to run for president, she wasn't happy. She asked me why I needed to take on such a time-consuming (read: waste of time, in her mind) job and reminded me how important my schoolwork was. I knew I could balance both, as well as playing in the spring musical in school. I was a good student and a very good time manager. And I was excited about having a leadership role in a group of other girls where I felt like I belonged, which I had never felt before, since I was the only Jewish student in my elementary, junior high, and high school.

Being elected president was a huge boost for my self-confidence and it was such an amazing feeling to know that other girls my age thought I was smart and competent. I never dreamed that Mutti would be so jealous of my peer acceptance and 'success' that she would sabotage it. But that she did.

Apparently, the strategy of taking away the car worked so well for Mutti that she used it again the next year, when I had a job at Hickory Farms at Washington Square. A fairly significant snowstorm swept through Portland the night before, but I had to get to work. I began to back out and down our steep, curving driveway. I felt the tires lose traction. I couldn't turn at the curve and then, the unmistakable sound of crumpling metal. I had hit the lava-rock retaining wall that bordered the driveway.

Mutti came out of the house screaming at me. "How could you be so stupid, Em?" she yelled, as she looked at the back of the light-blue car, currently dented and scratched by the sharp edges of the lava rock.

"Well, you're going to have to pay for the damage," Mutti continued. "And you're grounded from using the car."

I remember calling in sick to work because I was too embarrassed to tell them the truth. I honestly thought Mutti would calm down and see reason: if I couldn't use the car, then I couldn't go to work, which meant I couldn't make money to pay for the damage. But, she didn't. No amount of reasoning, pleading, or crying changed Mutti's mind. After three or four days of calling in sick, my manager called me and told me I was fired. Again, Mutti's flawed logic and punishment that didn't fit the crime (which wasn't really a crime, but "accidents happen" was not in Mutti's vocabulary).

I didn't see it then, but as an adult with 20/20 hindsight, I can tell it wasn't just the denial of material possessions or privileges that Mutti passed down to me as she experienced it from my grandfather (and those red shoes) and then the Nazi regime, it was also the shame of not fitting in or being accepted in the social group she wanted to join but couldn't. The fact that I had been elected to a leadership position in my youth group touched a raw nerve for her: she could not participate in and be a part of a youth group—or any other organization, in fact, she couldn't even finish high school—because she was Jewish and the Nazis were in power. They took every opportunity to belong to society as a whole away from the Jews, and Mutti made sure that I knew how that felt.

What's more, by taking away car privileges, Mutti could keep me nearby and dependent on her—and safe from the untrustworthy world. Conscious intent or not, this message was one I clearly received time and time again throughout my childhood.

YOUR TURN:

- Did your parent/grandparent want you (or your parent) to have more than they had and achieve greater success than they did, or did they want you to suffer because of their suffering in the Holocaust?

- Did you sense any other kind of jealousy by your parent of your 'normal' childhood in a free country?

- How did your parent/grandparent help or hinder your growth and achievements during your childhood?

- Were you subjected to over-the-top punishments or did your parent withhold privileges that seemed not to fit the situation? Or were you showered with gifts and encouraged at every turn?

- Was your parent/grandparent overprotective of you and distrustful of the world in general, only feeling comfortable around other Jews? Or did they embrace the world and reaffirm a belief that humans are, in general, good?

CHAPTER FOUR

The Fashion Police

"Hey, Kris. Those sundresses you posted on Facebook are so cute. Where'd you get them?" I asked.

"At eShakti.com. They size them to fit your measurements and are so reasonably priced. It's my go-to for adorable, easy dresses," Kris responded.

Since great-fitting sundresses have eluded me my entire life, I figure I'll give it a try. So, I click the link, anticipating being greeted by the fun florals, cheerful checks, and pretty paisleys I saw Kris post on her Facebook page.

Instead, my eyes were brutally accosted by an image of a long, dark grey or black dress with narrow white pinstripes. Most people would say, "Oh, what a lovely striped dress!" But not me. All I saw was the clothing worn by concentration camp prisoners. Slap on a yellow felt Star of David with the word "Jude" on the left side of the dress and the outfit would be complete.

Growing up with Mutti, vertically striped clothing was forbidden. In fact, we didn't have any striped fabrics in the house at all: Bed sheets were floral or paisley, if not plain. Curtains and upholstery were all solid colors. When Mutti kept my grandparents' striped sofa after Omi (my grandmother) passed away, I was shocked. I asked her about it and she said, "Well, the stripes are various widths, Em, not pinstripes." Omi and Opi (my grandfather) must have rationalized the sofa upholstery the same way, but I never asked.

One of the more extreme reaches of Mutti's stripe-free outlook extended to baseball. Not that Vati was a huge baseball—or any sports other than golf and bowling—fan, but he did watch the World Series every year. I would often join him (a foreshadowing of my later love of the game). But in the late '70s, specifically 1976, 1977, 1978, and again in 1981, Vati and I had to watch in utter secrecy, thanks to the New York Yankees' ubiquitous pin-striped uniforms.

While I had an aversion to the pinstripes myself (is this one of the reasons I'm a Boston Red Sox fan?) and have never, ever rooted for the Yankees, I could put that aside for my favorite sport. But Mutti would yell and then turn off the TV if she saw the pinstriped uniforms. Vati and I took to watching the games in which the Yankees played in the back bedroom, on a small black and white TV with the sound turned way down low.

Recently, I went to the Brooklyn Museum to see the Georgia O'Keeffe exhibit entitled "Living Modern." In addition to her major paintings and photographs, the exhibit focused on her wardrobe, including dresses and pantsuits designed and sewn by O'Keeffe herself.

In the exhibit, the first time that O'Keeffe's clothing has been seen outside Santa Fe, New Mexico, I could see that she paid the same attention to detail in her sewing as she did in her painting, but I couldn't help but be repulsed by the fabrics and dress styles, both of which were evocative of female concentration camp prisoners' clothing (a smock-type striped dress).

Given that O'Keeffe designed and sewed these dresses in the 1920's and 1930's—before the establishment of concentration camps—and in the United States, not in Germany or Poland, it's difficult to fathom that she was influenced by the "striped pajamas" of the Holocaust, or vice versa. What's more, because O'Keeffe was not Jewish nor did she have any relatives in Europe who had experienced the Holocaust first-hand, I'm fairly convinced that she didn't see a connection between her clothing and prisoners' garb, even later in life. It just wasn't part of her consciousness or that of most people, except Holocaust survivors and their progeny, like me.

Mutti's list of "verboten" (prohibited) clothing didn't stop at stripes. She simply didn't like color. At one point, I counted eight pairs of beige, six pairs of gray, and three pairs of white pants. All of her sweaters and t-shirts were beige, gray, taupe, off-white, and white. In her later years, Mutti did begin to sprinkle some periwinkle or light teal into her wardrobe, but the items were always muted, soft colors.

The reason I say verboten is because, as a child, I was subject to the same, strict color palette. And I hated it! I remember walking into the Brass Plum at Nordstrom for some back-to-school shopping with Mutti and pulling out item after item that was rejected: Purple! Orange! Black! Bright blue! Nein, nein, nein, nein. Again I came home with beige and taupe that, besides being boring, look awful on me, with my olive skin and dark hair.

As a trained seamstress, Mutti would often sew my clothes, but I had no say in the style or which Butterick or McCall's pattern she used. Besides the embarrassment I felt because, "Nobody else's mom sews their clothes, Mutti! Can't we just go shopping?" the colors were always her choice as well. Let me tell you how stunning I was in a rust-colored corduroy pantsuit in seventh grade. I just wanted to hide.

In retrospect, that's what Mutti was doing by choosing drab, light colors for her clothing: she was hiding, not calling attention to herself. And she was doing the same to me. In the concentration camp, you didn't want to do anything to attract the attention of the Nazi guards, you wanted to be as invisible as possible. The same theory held true for those survivors who managed to escape capture by going into hiding. By only wearing beige, tan, off-white, and other similar colors, she could continue to hide. And by forcing me to wear the same colors, she was ensuring that I didn't stand out, didn't attract unwanted attention.

The first thing I did when I got to Berkeley was to buy a pair of pink and black plaid pants.

Mutti's other clothing trigger was actually footwear, specifically clogs, which became fashionable (again) when I was in high school in the early 1980s. Desperate to 'fit in' and wear what all the other girls were wearing, I came home from school one day asking for a pair of clogs. While I had heard Mutti's stories of digging trenches and graves in the snow wearing wooden clogs for years, I didn't make the connection with my teenage self's desires. And the fact that the 'fashion police' dictated that the clogs were to be worn without socks, just as she had worn in camp, made her reaction that much worse.

"Ach, Em! How can you wear those? I had to wear them in the snow and the snow would stick to the bottom of the clog and pile up. Every few steps, I had to stop and knock off the snow or I would roll my ankles," I remember Mutti saying. "That's why my ankles are so bad now, because they got weak from wearing clogs in the snow."

There was no way Mutti was going to allow me to wear clogs, let alone give me the money to buy a pair. So, I did what any enterprising teen did when her mother said no to an item that would significantly affect her social standing: I saved up my babysitting money and bought them secretly, stashing them in my locker at school. This scenario repeated itself a year or two later, when Mutti forbid me from wearing the ubiquitous Candies sandals, the spikey high-heeled ankle breakers with the faux wooden soles that made me feel like I was walking on stilts. Even though they didn't look remotely like a clog, at least to me, and the soles were not real wood, Mutti wouldn't hear of it.

YOUR TURN:

- Did your parent/grandparent have triggers about certain types of clothes?
- Did they tend to wear drab colors or bright colors and bold prints?
- Did they put any restrictions on what you wore?
- Can you tie those triggers or restrictions to their Holocaust experience?

CHAPTER FIVE

Leaving on a Jet Plane

Tomorrow, I board a flight to Minneapolis. It's the Friday before Christmas and snow is in the forecast. I shake. I come up with a slew of excuses not to go; some of them real, some of them complete fabrications. It's a friend's wedding. I should go. I need to go. But I want to cancel. I want to find any reason not to go.

What if the plane crashes on the way there? What if the plane crashes on the way home? What if I'm stuck there for two or three or even four days? What if I never make it home?

I'm only describing one day in my life, but I've felt this anxiety so many times. It always unfolds the same way: I'm excited about the trip when it's just an idea, a plane reservation, a hotel booking. Something nebulous in the future. As the trip date approaches, I watch the weather closely. If there's a snowstorm, a hurricane, or any other major weather event in the forecast, my anxiety level spikes even higher each day before departure. For most people, this would cause concern but they would reason through it and say, "Whatever happens, happens." But me? I hyperventilate every time I think about the trip, my hands perspire, and my thoughts are consumed with all the things that could go wrong, from minor delays and inconveniences to death. Sometimes, I even vomit due to nerves.

Once I'm on the plane, the nerves subside. Especially if I am traveling with someone else. The anxiety is much more acute when I am traveling alone. Just getting to the airport can be a serious exercise in mind over mind and sheer inertia, because I often cry uncontrollably and become extremely emotional in the final hours of packing, which makes everything take longer, and then I run late—causing more anxiety and stress. Completely counterproductive, I know, but I simply can't help it.

As long as I can remember, I have battled travel anxiety. It definitely worsened once I had my children. And then again when Mutti became unable to care for herself and moved into an assisted living facility. I was petrified to go on a business trip or vacation in the event that something might happen to her and I couldn't get back.

The worst attack I can remember happened when my husband's father died and we had to fly to West Virginia for the funeral. Mutti was visiting from Seattle—it was Hanukkah—and our flight left before hers. In fact, she had to get to Oakland airport on her own (we flew out of SFO) and, even though she was mobile, I wasn't sure she would get the details of her flight right. The last time I visited her in Seattle, Mutti had mixed up my flight number and the arrival time, leaving me at the airport, frantically wondering where she was and whether I should go to her apartment. Would we cross paths on the freeway, her driving south to Sea-Tac and me going north in a taxi? Oh, how I wish I had had a cell phone back then.

I can still see myself in my living room in Berkeley having a full-on panic attack. I couldn't calm myself down or reason with myself. I couldn't catch my breath. Heaving sobs wracked my entire body. I couldn't stop long enough to articulate what I was afraid of. In the end, everything turned out fine, but I didn't relax until Mutti called me to tell me she had made it home to Seattle safely.

I know the genesis of this anxiety: Mutti never wanted me going anywhere without her, especially not if it involved traveling any distance. From somewhere as close to my house as a Girl Scout camp overnight in third grade or as far as a girls' road trip to Southern California after a college semester at Cal, Mutti would talk about all the 'bad things' that could happen to me. I remember when I decided to attend Cal, Mutti said, "Over my dead body!"–She wanted me to go to the University of Oregon or the University of Washington so I could come home every weekend and she could drop in on me unexpectedly–but I managed to convince her to let me go. I was, however, subjected to her certainty that I would die in a demonstration on Sproul Plaza.

Even deciding to go to Cal was somewhat driven by my travel anxiety. Berkeley was certainly closer than the East Coast, where I had been admitted to an Ivy League college. But in April of 1982, when I had to make my college decision, Vati had a stroke. I started to worry that I couldn't get home from the East Coast if something happened to him–or get back to school if I were home in

Portland. So, I elected to stay on the West Coast where, if push came to shove, I could drive home in less than a day.

Mutti's descriptions of the 'bad world' from which she wanted to protect me filled me with "what-if" statements, from the time I was a little girl. Often, she would allow me to participate in an activity after I begged and pleaded—and after she told me about all the awful things that might or could happen. I would feel proud of myself for convincing Mutti to let me go, only to feel despair and fear once I actually arrived at the destination. I would feel so scared that I had to get home—pronto. In effect, Mutti created my homesickness.

I remember being really excited about going to summer camp at Camp Solomon Schechter for two weeks in the summer after third grade. I had enlisted Vati's help in convincing Mutti to let me go. I got to camp, settled into my bunk, and went to see the list of activities. Unfortunately, Mutti had not signed the release forms allowing me to do the two most fun—and most talked about—activities: water skiing and horseback riding. She had told me this in advance, but I thought she'd change her mind and let me 'fit in' with the others. Silly me. So, while everyone else enjoyed the water and the horses, I whiled away my time alone in the cabin, reading. One week in, I felt so left out that I wanted to go home. And I did: I called home and asked Mutti and Vati to come pick me up. Mutti's first words when they arrived at camp? "See? I told you that you wouldn't like it."

Today, because I accept this anxiety and understand its roots, I am in more control of my reactions. I still enjoy the planning stages of a trip more than the packing and preparation—and then physically getting to the airport—phases, and I have to talk myself through the last few days before I leave, but it's definitely improving. I've only canceled a trip at the last-minute once in the last six months and I'm happily planning a few more this year, which I intend to take. And I hope I don't hyperventilate too much.

YOUR TURN:

- Can you remember a time that you felt scared or anxious of an event or situation?
- What can you recall from your childhood about how your parents might have instilled you with that fear?

- How have you tried to overcome your fear or anxiety? Has it been successful? Why or why not?
- Are there clear connections to your parent's/grandparent's Holocaust experience?

Chapter Six

Head Games

"Em, you're fat. Look at that tuchas. You take after your father's family, not mine."

"Mutti, I'm bored." "Em, only stupid children are bored."

"Mutti, I'm tired." "Em, sure you're tired. Spelled F-A-U-L." (Faul is lazy in German)

"No amount of make-up will make that face pretty, Em."

When I wasn't dealing with physical abuse by fly swatter, I was ducking, avoiding, and evading emotional and verbal abuse. I cannot remember a time that Mutti paid me a compliment or provided positive reinforcement.

Heaven forbid I came home from school with a story of a disagreement with a friend or being bullied by someone in the neighborhood, like the time another girl on the middle school bus beat me up because I was Jewish (her words, not mine). Walking into the house, nose bloody, arms bruised, I found Mutti in the living room.

"What happened?" Mutti asked.

"A girl on the bus hit and punched me," I replied.

"What did you do to provoke her? It must be your fault." Mutti's message to me was clear: everyone else was good and right and I was bad and wrong. And if I would say something wasn't fair, watch out.

Nothing I ever complained or felt upset about could compare to what Mutti had gone through in the Holocaust, and she made sure that I never forgot that. The Holocaust and her trauma dominated our house and I felt constantly measured against her—and her parents' (my grandparents) martyrdom and courage. Compared to Mutti's strength and determination to survive, nothing I could do would ever be good enough. I failed to measure up to an unattainable standard before I even started trying.

But I did try. And the struggle for acceptance, love, and being told I was worthy and 'good enough' extended to how I dealt with friendships as a child and young adult. Because I didn't have the essential unconditional love of a parent that leads a child to have self-esteem, I went looking for that validation from others. I couldn't bear being left out of an activity that friends had organized (an early example of FOMO?). If two friends were going to the movies and I hadn't been included, I would feel desperate and worthless. I would sob for hours and then get angry with my friends, often calling them to berate them for not including me. You can imagine how that turned out.

My need to be included and "loved" extended into my college years and beyond. Joining a sorority was the best thing I did during college to feel a sense of security and belonging. Those women are my close friends to this day but, even within that group, I had feelings of being the outsider. I remember a party that one of my sorority sisters threw and I had not been invited. I called her, upset, and she said, "Emily, not everyone gets invited to everything." "Well, why the hell not?" I thought. And I wasn't everyone, dammit.

Yes, I looked for love in all the wrong places for many years after college, trying to force intimate relationships or extend them longer than their shelf life. The wrong guys. A**holes. Men who didn't treat me with respect. Ones who were emotionally unavailable. This all makes sense now: I didn't think I deserved respect because I wasn't good enough, smart enough, or pretty enough. My extremely high tolerance for pain—and oh, was it high—led me to allow people to treat me terribly and I thought I deserved it. I managed. I was so used to living in 'that place' that it was normal to me.

"Chasing love" is how someone recently put it. The intense desire to be loved, hugged, cherished, adored by someone to make you feel "good enough" or "worthy." Many 2Gs can relate to having a Holocaust survivor parent who could not say "I love you," never gave hugs or kisses, and never expressed affection in any way. This surely correlates directly to the fact that, in the Holocaust, they could not get attached to anything, material or human, because material things were taken away and family members were snatched by the Nazis, never to return.

In business, too, I tolerated terrible treatment, although others were not as traumatized by those individuals as I was because of my history. When the CEO of a company I worked for yelled, "You're an embarrassment to the company" for explaining standard PR protocol, or completely ignored my professional advice in a crisis communications situation, I would get extremely angry, consumed with feelings of disrespect and questions like "Why doesn't anyone believe me?" "Why can't I be respected?" Everything felt like a personal attack when, in reality, it was probably not about me, but rather about *his* feelings of inadequacy and need for attention. Co-workers would tell me to ignore it, let it go, don't get so upset, but I simply couldn't. It was a trigger for me, thanks to Mutti's transferred trauma.

Even in my marriage and with my family, I kept looking for external validation of my worth. I also realized how much like my mother my husband was, not in terms of physical abuse, but the lack of positive reinforcement and support, the aversion to change, the control over decisions, and the emotional unavailability. As my awareness of Mutti's transmitted trauma increased, so did my discomfort in the constraints of a marriage that felt more like a parent (him) and child (me) relationship than a partnership.

When my husband would say, "Don't forget to wipe the dog's paws," on a rainy day, I would explode. If I wanted or needed something in the house, say a ceiling fan or a fridge, he decided when we would buy it, even though both of us had jobs and incomes. I increasingly felt that I was trapped and living with my mother again, who controlled every aspect of my childhood and continued to be a huge influence in my life and on my self-esteem until her death.

The feeling of being on the outside looking in permeated every aspect of my life, with parents of my children's classmates and teammates, with my tennis teams, with other couples with whom we would socialize. I continued to feel desperate for inclusion and acceptance. I would join a group, get excited that "this time it'll be different," and it just never was. I never felt part of the "inner circle." Then the lack of self-esteem and sense of unworthiness would wash over me. Why am I not good enough? Why can't I be important? Why doesn't that group include me? I kept reliving Mutti's transferred trauma over and over.

Because I wasn't strong enough on my own to leave my marriage, in which I felt shackled, I made another bad choice: I got involved with a man who didn't respect me (or any woman, to be honest), who treated me poorly, who emotionally, verbally, and physically abused me—and I still wanted him to love me. How low can your self-esteem be when a man physically injures you, calls you the worst names in the world, tells you that you are pathetic, worthless, weak, ugly, stupid, and fat, and you *still* think you can make him love you? I am paying for that decision and will continue to pay for it for a long time, in many ways.

But what that awful relationship did teach me, finally, was that no one else is responsible for my self-esteem and feelings of self-worth but me. Mutti clearly didn't feel worthy of love or "good enough" due to the trauma she experienced in the Holocaust, and she, in turn, made sure that I felt the same. But now, I know that love starts with me.

I also now recognize that I cultivated friendships with other women who behaved like Mutti. Why? Again, because it was my "comfort zone" to be derided and questioned. It's quite a wake-up call when you realize that, no matter what your accomplishment or achievement, your "friend" finds something negative to say or tells you what you did isn't that big of a deal. Whether it's misery loves company or just simple mean-spiritedness, I now have no tolerance for that behavior. I am slowly kicking those people off my elevator as I rise to the higher floors of happiness.

YOUR TURN:

- Did your parent/grandparent openly express affection? Did they hug you freely or avoid physical touch at all costs?
- Did they say "I love you" easily and often or do you have a difficult time remembering any specific instance when they said those three words?
- How do you respond to physical affection in your relationships? Do you let your loved ones know that you love them—both verbally and physically—or do you hold back, keeping those emotions tamped down inside of you?
- Do you get involved with the wrong romantic partners or platonic friends because of an overwhelming sense of insecurity and lack of self-worth?
- Do you often feel excluded, like you don't fit in? Are you desperate to be seen as "normal" and be included in group activities?

CHAPTER SEVEN

Food for Thought

Whenever I see canned pears, I am immediately transported into my grandparents' apartment in Seattle, Washington. Apartment 202, across from the Rosenbergs and down the hall from Mrs. Thalheimer.

I'm in the kitchen with Omi making Birnen und Klöße for dinner, my favorite dish. We're making Semelklöße, the bread dumplings, for the dish. The rolls are soaking in milk. The canned pears, the Birnen, are on the counter.

When I was young, Mutti and I would take the Greyhound bus from Portland to Seattle, and back again, several times a year. Each time, Omi would ask me what I wanted for dinner the first night. I never wavered: "Birnen und Klöße bitte!!!!!"

My grandfather, Opi, would pick us up at the bus station in his 1968 Plymouth Valiant and drive us to their apartment. Upon walking into the building, I would be greeted with the unmistakable smell of 733 Summit Avenue East: a mix of moth balls, chicken soup, and the variety of perfumes worn by the many elderly Jewish women who lived in the building, including Omi's 4711 cologne.

I'd excitedly run down the hall and to the right, straight to Apartment 202, while Mutti and Opi walked slowly behind me with the luggage. The door would already be open, an indicator that Omi was eagerly anticipating our arrival. I would push open the door and run straight to the kitchen, where Omi would be surrounded with all the ingredients for my favorite dish.

Sometimes, the smell of "Omi Cookies," the sinfully rich butter cookies with Vanillienzucker (Vanilla sugar) sprinkled on top, would be in the air. I would try to stuff as many of my favorite cookies into my mouth as possible, while Omi simultaneously warned against ruining my dinner.

Once the Birnen und Klöße were cooking in the pot, it would be time to set the table—and to take Opi's beer out of the refrigerator. Opi liked his beer—always dark, usually a Henry Weinhard's—at room temperature, so it had to come out of the fridge and be put on the table an hour before dinner. I'm sure he liked it that way because that's how it was served in Germany in the '20s and '30s, when he was a young man, but why it was in the fridge in the first place always confused me. I never asked, though.

I set the table with Omi's Corelle ware dishes with the gold pattern. A beer glass for Opi, tiny juice glasses for Omi and Mutti, and a tall plastic Tupperware cup for me, for my soda. I didn't notice until many years later that soda loses its carbonation faster in plastic than in glass, but I remember thinking, "Why is the soda in Seattle always flat?"

The next night, Omi would make my second-favorite meal: pork tenderloin studded with bacon, served with potato dumplings and sour cream sauce. (What's with my obsession with dumplings?) The only way this meal could be more un-Kosher is if Omi had put in shrimp as well!

Mutti tried to replicate this dish after Omi died, but it never tasted quite the same. Even when I make it now, it feels like it's missing something. Likely because Omi didn't use recipes and when Mutti or I asked her to write it down, she'd invariably forget an ingredient.

But none of these dishes could compare with Omi's Schokoladenfisch (chocolate fish), which she made every December. A Silesian specialty traditionally served during the Christmas holiday season, I could not WAIT to cut into that yummy chocolate fish with marzipan in the center. After Omi passed away, Mutti continued to make it every year, and I now make it every year as well. Often, I play with the recipe, adding variety to the nuts and dried fruit in the chocolate. It's so good that it really shouldn't be restricted to the winter holidays.

While Omi would always make my favorite meals when I visited, Mutti stuck to the traditional German foods my father enjoyed. In other words, it was a lucky day for me if we had chicken or a flank steak. "Normal food," as I called it back then. What I really meant was, "I cannot invite a friend over for dinner or I will die. This is disgusting!"

My father's favorite meal was beef tongue, pickled and served whole on a wooden carving board. You could almost imagine the cow that owned the tongue, sticking it out to lick something right on that board. If you like tongue, which I didn't, the best part is the tip (or Spitze) of the tongue not the back, which is more fatty. Me? I didn't want to have ANYTHING to do with tongue back then, and Mutti's lack of presentation skills didn't help much. Salty and with a soft, mushy texture that didn't say meat to my American taste buds, I just could not eat tongue. [Now, I LOVE a good tongue and chopped liver sandwich!]

There were only two dinners I disliked more than tongue. The first was Sülze, or headcheese, with its indistinguishable pieces of pork in some kind of jelly. Served cold and with vinegar (to mask the horrendous taste of the jelly?) along with warm potato salad, the headcheese would wiggle on the plate like Jell-O when you bumped the table. Vati loved this meal, and we usually had it the day he would go to the German butcher on the east side of Portland. On the rare occasion that I would go to the butcher with him, I'd spend my time picking out my favorite chocolates: the Sprüngli Stäbchen, chocolate sticks with liquid orange and lemon inside (I could eat an entire box at one sitting) and chocolate-covered marzipan.

The other meal I dreaded was Mutti's kohlrabi stew, which she made not only with the root vegetable itself but also with its leaves and beef stew meat. Dark green is a color that should be reserved for vegetable side dishes, not a stew. And when you ate this stew, your poop turned dark green for days. Truly awful. (There will be NO recipe to download for that disgusting stew!)

On the other hand, when I was sick, there was nothing better than Mutti's Milchreis (milk rice). Milchreis is a simple preparation of long-grain white rice cooked in milk then topped with cinnamon and sugar. It's similar to rice pudding and oh-so-yummy when you have a cold or the flu. Sometimes, Mutti would make a geschlagenes Ei (whipped raw egg), which is just whipped egg white with an egg yolk folded in for color and sugar. Although I didn't love it, I did eat it on occasion when nothing else sounded or looked appetizing due to illness.

Even lunchtime sandwiches had rules: the proportion of meat and cheese to bread had to be less than 1:1, meaning piling a sandwich high with turkey or pastrami was forbidden. As was my occasional sneak of a piece of cheese or a slice of salami without ANY bread. When I got caught, the fly swatter came out. Clearly, this rule can be traced back to the scarcity of food in concentration camp and the post-war years.

At the time, I didn't really think twice about the fact that we were a Jewish family but most of the dishes we ate were more identifiable as German rather than Jewish cuisine, which meant a lot of pork. Neither of my parents was particularly religious, and from all indications, their families were not particularly religious either, and they didn't keep kosher back in Germany.

Now I believe that this was representative of how many Jews in Germany felt during the rise of Hitler: they identified as Germans first, Jews second. I have read that this self-identification is why many Jews didn't feel that Hitler was a threat, or that their non-Jewish German friends would protect them. They were, after all, Germans too.

While Mutti was observant in other ways, going to synagogue on High Holidays and Yahrzeits and keeping Passover and Hanukkah, Vati wanted very little to do with organized religion or anything he felt pressured to do. Every year on Yom Kippur, Vati would mysteriously come down with a fever or stomach ailment, so he wouldn't have to go to shul. Mutti would let Vati get out of shul, but not me.

I remember being so envious of Vati getting to stay home, because Mutti didn't just go for one or two hours, it was an all-day affair. Invariably, Vati would be eating a ham and cheese or something else equally as un-kosher. On Yom Kippur, the Day of Atonement, when Jews are supposed to fast. My theory on why he would feign illness is that he couldn't stand to go without eating all day.

Last year, the first High Holidays without Mutti, I was feeling pressured by my family to go to temple. All the memories of Mutti making me go came flooding back and I really didn't want to go—at all.

"I don't feel well," I said. "I think I'll stay in bed." And I snuck a ham and cheese sandwich for lunch.

YOUR TURN:

- What was the role of food in your house?
- Did any rules about food (e.g., no eating meat or cheese without bread) or forbidden food items (e.g., lettuce because that was what was fed to the animals on their farm in the Old Country) exist?

- Did your parent keep Kosher in their home country? Did that change or stay the same after emigrating to the U.S. (or other country)?
- Did the foods you now consider "comfort food" tend toward the country of your parent's birth or toward traditional Jewish food?
- How religiously observant was your parent (and his/her family) before the Holocaust? Did this change in the years after?
- Was there pressure to attend synagogue and be strongly Jewish-identified or did your parent let you make your own choices?

You can find all the recipes mentioned in this chapter, and more, on my website at www.fromgentogenbook.com/recipes

CHAPTER EIGHT

Oh Brother, Who Art Thou?

The plain white envelope sat on the counter for two hours before I dared to open it. Technically, it wasn't mine to open: addressed to Mutti at her previous assisted living facility and forwarded to me at my house in Berkeley. But Mutti had advanced dementia and couldn't make a decision about opening an envelope, let alone comprehending its contents.

At first, I thought it might be junk mail camouflaged to look real, because both the sender's and recipient's addresses had been applied to the envelope using an antiquated machine called a typewriter. Just when I decided that it must be junk, I noticed a single, handwritten word in the lower left-hand corner of the envelope: "Personal."

With a postmark of Spokane, Washington and a return address in Spangle, Washington (where was that, anyway?), the contents of the envelope and the sender's identity gnawed at me while I cooked dinner and watched the results of the 2012 U.S. Presidential Election. "Who is Dianne Sams?" "How does she know Mutti?" "DOES she really know Mutti?" "What could she possibly want?"

While I was browning the chicken in my sauté pan, I decided. I would open it. I put the chicken and potatoes in the oven, took a deep breath, and sat down at the kitchen table. Carefully, I opened the envelope and pulled out the tri-fold letter inside. I remember thinking that I should steam it open so I could reseal it if I decided to give it to Mutti. Along with her dementia came some paranoia, and I didn't want her upset that I had opened a letter addressed to her. All of that thinking was ridiculous, though, because she was not able to process anything so complicated. I put the letter on the table and read:

Dear Hannelore:

My name is Dianne Sams. I am a Confidential Intermediary for the Superior Court State of Washington.

I am contacting you on behalf of a man who was born in Aberdeen, Washington on October 15, 1948 to Hannelore Lorraine (Breitkopf) Jacobson. Your birth son is not trying to hurt you or hassle you or your family in any way. However, he would like to have the opportunity to know you, and give you the opportunity to know him.

I have a letter and picture that he would like to share with you.

I realize that this is a great shock, and may, indeed, take some time. However, I do hope you will consider this and take advantage of it. Please contact me at your earliest convenience to discuss this further. You are welcome to call collect. Hope to hear from you soon.

Sincerely,

Dianne Sams

By the time I reached the end of the letter, I'm not sure I was breathing. I was stunned. This is impossible, I thought. It's a mistake. Maybe even a cruel joke.

I thought back to all the times I asked Mutti if I had an older brother or sister. Since both of my parents had been married before (once each, I thought, until I found out about Mutti's first husband, Peter, when I was an older teenager), and Mutti was 42 and Vati was 56 when I was born, I figured there was a good possibility that at least one of them had had a child in a previous marriage that they weren't telling me about. But when I asked, the answer was always no.

One time, when I was about 13 and we were talking about the sibling topic, Mutti told me that she had gotten pregnant again after I was born, but that she had miscarried. I remember asking her if she knew if the baby was a boy or a girl, and she replied that she "thought" it had been a boy.

Looking back, I wonder if she was acknowledging the baby born in 1948 but changing the timeline to suit her narrative. A miscarriage stops the conversation. Altering the timeframe helped her hide the pain—and the humiliation—she must have felt. She also knew that this was not something I would bring up with my father, so her lie would not be exposed, at least not during his life-time.

I kept staring at the birthdate in the letter: October 15th. October 15th was always a noteworthy date in our family. My grandfather, Opi, was born on October 15th, as was my Onkel Ken, and both of them were so terribly stubborn that when one of them did or said something that smacked of stubbornness, the rest of us would look at each other and say, "October 15th. What can you do?" We always had a good laugh over that.

The year of birth also caught my eye. As far as I knew, in 1948, Mutti was living with her parents on a farm owned by Omi's brother, Onkel Fritz. Onkel Fritz's son and their black and white English Springer Spaniel, Beau, were also living there. Had Mutti been pregnant while living in a house with three other adults, wouldn't everyone—or at least someone—have noticed? And if she were absent on Opi's birthday, for whatever reason, wouldn't her absence have been cause for concern or suspicion?

Election returns forgotten, I called a few friends, hoping that one of them would see a detail that I didn't, notice something—anything—that would explain this letter away. Instead, all I got was the same sense of disbelief and shock that I felt.

Later that evening, I emailed Onkel Fritz's son to see if he could shed any light on this new development. Mutti stopped speaking with him after he kicked Beau, the dog, when she was living with them in Aberdeen. I always thought that was an odd reason to completely cut off ties with someone and figured there was more to the story, but I never pried. Mutti was not someone with whom you could discuss anything and get a deeper, more satisfying answer or get her to realize that she was wrong.

The minute I sent the email, I regretted it. What if his response included something I wasn't ready to deal with? But the next morning, when I opened his email, his response actually raised more questions than it provided answers.

"I returned to my father from the farm where he had boarded me for 7 years in 1946 or 1947. We all lived in the same house. I was never aware of your mother being pregnant. She was a slim woman and I think it would have been evident. Nor did I hear of a baby. The only people I met in the house were your mom, Erna, and Al. I do not know when they left for Seattle and I do not know

what went on there. But I think it was after 1948. I have never heard of a baby."

I set the email exchange aside and refocused on the letter. I still had the option of throwing it away and not following up on its contents. I could pretend it never existed and continue on with my life, just as Mutti had done. It occurred to me that one of the reasons Mutti and I always had a strained relationship was that we were polar opposites: I typically would react or do the exact opposite of her. We really didn't understand each other's thought processes. This situation was no different. Mutti would have thrown away the letter and put the baby behind her once again. Me? I needed to unravel the mystery—or at least scratch the surface of it.

Later that morning, the sun streaming through the windows, I sat on my bed and called the Washington State Adoption Records Department. In a lovely and gentle voice, the woman who answered the phone said she could tell me if there was a file with my mom's name, but she could not tell me its contents.

As I explained the situation and gave Mutti's name, I expected her to say, "No sorry, we have no information about Hannelore Breitkopf."

Instead, she asked me who sent the letter and, when I told her, said, "Dianne is very reputable and does her research. She doesn't send these letters unless she is sure she's right," she replied. She then put me on hold. For a long time. (At least it seemed that way).

When she finally came back to the phone, she said, "Yes, there's a file here for your mom."

I immediately felt faint. I could hear my heart beating loudly. If anyone else had been in the room, they probably would have heard it too.

I thanked her, hung up the phone, and barely made it to the bathroom to vomit. Now I knew that this was not something I could ignore.

My biggest problem was that I couldn't simply show Mutti the letter and ask her about its contents: her dementia was too advanced. Even if that weren't the case, she probably would have denied the entire thing even as she held the letter in her hand and looked me in the eye. I'm certain she would have said, "Sie lügt" (she lies) as she ripped up the piece of paper into tiny pieces.

A few days later, I called Dianne Sams. She answered on the first ring. I explained why her letter to Mutti was in my hands. Then I bombarded her with all my questions.

First and foremost, I wanted to know who was listed as the father on the birth certificate.

"Peter Jacobson," Dianne said.

I knew Peter, Mutti's first husband, couldn't possibly be the father, because Mutti told me that he died in the concentration camp. Dianne confirmed that Peter was not on the registry of passengers for the U.S.S. Marine Perch in 1946 with my mom and grandparents in 1946— and not on any other ship registry from Germany to the U.S. in the years after the war. Nor did she find him in any U.S. immigration database.

By signing the form included with the letter and returning it to Dianne, she would send me a copy of the birth certificate, along with a letter from and a recent photo of the man claiming to be Mutti's son. Then she would tell me his current name and contact information— and would give him mine.

I hung up, more confused than before. Did I really want to find out more? Who was this man and what did he want from Mutti? Why did he wait so long to contact her? Did I really want to meet or talk with him? Was it even my right or prerogative to trespass on Mutti's past? There was a reason she never told me about this, so who was I to go digging?

My entire life I had wished for a sibling and now here he was. And I wasn't sure I wanted him.

For the next few days, while I debated whether or not to sign and return the consent form, I obsessed over the question of who was the father of my half-brother? If it wasn't Peter, which I knew for sure, then who?

I eventually came to the conclusion that I really didn't need to know this information, after a long discussion with my rabbi. After two hours discussing the letter, Mutti, and the baby—who was now a 64-year-old man—my rabbi said, "Emily, do you really want to know? Because, as I see it, none of the options are positive."

He listed the options as he saw them: Mutti could have been raped by a stranger. Or coerced into sex with a boss or coworker. Maybe it was incest. Or possibly it was a lover who left her.

The rabbi was right. None of the viable options for the baby's father were positive. All of them meant sadness and pain for Mutti. Did I really want to find out, for example, that someone she worked for or with had taken advantage of her? Or did I want to know that she had been raped by a stranger—or worse, by her uncle?

After a weekend of debating with myself, I decided to sign the release form. I still didn't know what I hoped for, just that I wanted to know more. Would I have anything in common with him? Would we look at all alike? Would I be able to forge a relationship with him? And did I really want to?

Within five minutes of hitting "Send," my phone rang. I could see on the Caller ID that it was Dianne. I let it ring a couple more times, took a deep breath, and picked up the phone.

"Are you ready to find out who your half-brother is?" Dianne asked.

YOUR TURN:

- Have you discovered any secrets, either from war times or afterward, that your parent hid from you?
- Did they keep the truth from other family members as well? Or were other family members in on the cover-up?
- Was it a secret that you had never even contemplated, a complete blindside or did your parent drop hints?
- Was your discovery of the truth a proactive effort on your part, or did a third party force you to face the fact?

CHAPTER NINE

From Poland with Love

Ria and her grandson, Matheus, took us to the back room. "Here," she said, "is where my father hid his workbelt and tools from the Nazis. He opened up the wall, put in the tools, and closed up the wall again. And then we fled."

I had always known about the Nazis' impact on my Jewish family, most of whom perished in the concentration camps. But I had never heard of nor did I expect to find out about an impact on my Catholic relatives, my grandfather's family in Poland and Germany. I had no idea that they had to flee their homes, pushed out and to the east to Russia by the Nazis.

Ria's family was lucky. After the war, they were able to come back to their hometown of Opole, Poland, to a standing house. It was the farmhouse in which my grandfather and his 11 siblings, including Ria's mother, Albertine, had grown up. A classic Polish farmhouse: square with no real landscaping. From what I heard that day, many of their neighbors returned home to find nothing where their house formerly stood, thanks to the pillaging by the Nazis.

I wanted to ask Ria more questions about her experiences during World War II, her family's flight to Russia, and their return to Poland, but she was already excitedly walking back to the dining room to set up for tea and cake. I made a mental note to ask her later.

We all sat around Ria's oval table, which was covered in a yellow tablecloth: My German cousins, Achim, Uta, and Christine, on one side, my Polish ones on the other. Conversations in two different languages, neither of which was my native tongue. Luckily, I could participate in the German conversation, since Mutti had made sure I spoke German—learning it even before I spoke English.

After hearing about Ria's daily bike rides into town for groceries–no small feat for a frail woman of 85 with glaucoma!–over two types of cake and lots of tea, Ria motioned to me.

"Come with me upstairs. I have some pictures to show you," she said in German. I glanced at Achim, hoping he would come with me, in case I needed help with my German or to identify other relatives, but he made no move to get up from his chair.

As I followed Ria up the narrow stairs, I remember thinking, "I wonder which of these rooms was Opi's when he was a child?" That thought was immediately replaced with, "What will I do if Ria falls?" as she tripped on a stair and I reached out to keep her upright.

At the top of the stairs, Ria turned left, into what appeared to be a sitting room.

"Sit down here, on the sofa, while I get the photo albums," Ria said.

I complied and sat down on the sofa, which was old and sagging. The upholstery looked worn and sad, the pink and red flowers no longer vivid, the white background long grayed with age.

"Here are pictures of your mother and Peter," Ria said, as she opened up an old brown photo album filled with

black and white photos held in place with those obso-
lete little silver photo corners. The photos were taken at
a wedding, and Mutti and her first husband, Peter, were
in the wedding party.

Mutti and Peter married in December 1943, shortly
before they were both picked up by the Nazis and sent
to concentration camp. I can't remember exactly when
I first heard about Peter, but I know it was when I was
an older teen. I remember sitting on the sofa in our living room in Portland; Mutti was sitting on the coffee table when she told me. In contrast to when I found out
about Mutti's second husband—who I long thought was
her first—when I was nine years old, thanks to my cousin's
family tree project, this revelation didn't send me to my
room shrieking and sobbing. I just felt stunned to find
out that Mutti had been married *three* times!

The first picture I had ever seen of Peter was in their
wedding photo, a photo that my cousin Achim had
scanned in and sent me by email the year before our
visit to Ria. Mutti and Peter looked so young (they were
both 21, born in 1922). Mutti was wearing long, white
gloves and a beautiful dress I was sure she designed and
sewed herself, since she had trained as a seamstress in
Germany. Peter was wearing a top hat and tails, and he

was very handsome. Two very attractive young people with their lives in front of them. Unfortunately, the Third Reich changed everything.

Mutti and Peter's wedding, December 11th, 1943

"And here is a postcard that Peter and Hannelore sent me for my 13th birthday," Ria said as she flipped a page of the photo album. "You know, they were both always laughing and having fun. Your mother was so full of life—and she was funny!"

Postcard from Mutti and Peter to Ria on her 13th birthday

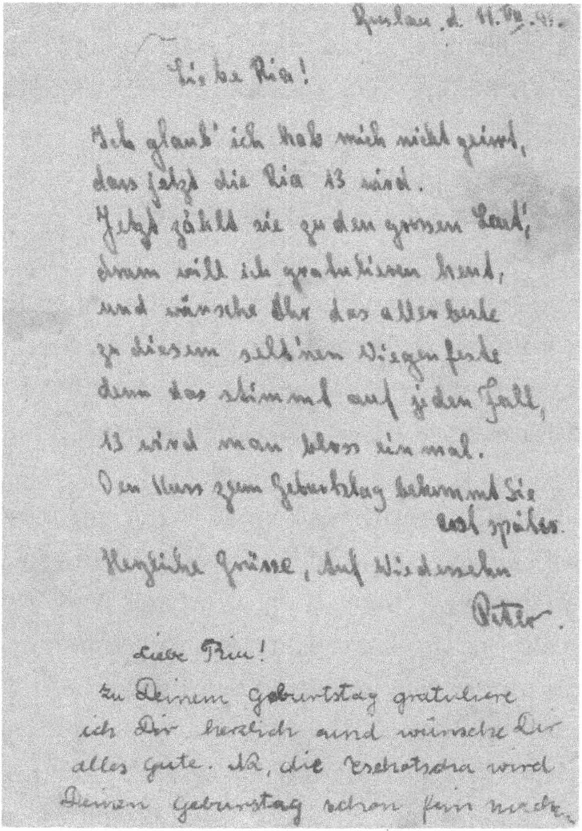
Breslau, d. 11.VII.41.

Liebe Ria!

Ich glaub' ich hab mich nicht geirrt,
dass jetzt die Ria 13 wird.
Jetzt zählt sie zu den grossen Leut',
drum will ich gratulieren heut,
und wünsche Dir das allerbeste
zu diesem seltenen Wiegenfeste
denn das stimmt auf jeden Fall,
13 wird man bloss einmal.
Den Kuss zum Geburtstag bekommst Sie
erst später.

Herzliche Grüsse, Auf Wiedersehn
Peter.

Liebe Ria!
Zu Deinem Geburtstag gratuliere
ich Dir herzlich und wünsche Dir
alles Gute. Na, die Tschatscha wird
Deinen Geburtstag schon fein mach...

Postcard from Mutti and Peter to Ria on her 13th birthday

Ria was painting a picture of a woman I didn't know. My mother full of life? Laughing? Having fun? I couldn't reconcile the woman Ria described with the Mutti I knew for 50 years.

I pulled the postcard out of the photo corners and tried to read what Peter and Mutti wrote. I recognized my mother's handwriting, but only barely, noting how it had morphed into the beautiful, curvy European handwriting I knew from my childhood. The capital "H" she used in her signature was the same, but the rest of the letters seemed smaller, less fluid, more tightly packed than I remember.

Still, I could easily read what Mutti had written to Ria—and I could read what Peter had written as well. As Ria said, they were funny! Both comments were light and humorous—and apparently unaware (or in denial?) of the evil and torture that would envelop them in just a few short months.

As I handled the postcard, Ria asked, "Would you like to have that? I'll give it to you if you want it. It means more to you than it does to me at this point in my life."

Did I want it? Of course, I wanted it! "I would love to have it, Ria. Thank you!"

I continued to flip the pages of the photo album. My eyes glanced over photo after photo of gatherings of people—weddings, sendoffs to war, other events I couldn't place.

I closed the photo album and turned to face Ria on the sofa. "It's just so sad that Peter died in concentration camp," I said.

"No, he didn't," came Ria's reply.

Three words that I never expected to hear. Peter didn't die? In every retelling of her Holocaust story, the narrative was the same: "I heard that the Russians were coming. I saw a chance to escape in the chaos. Peter came to visit me in the infirmary, where I was recovering from diphtheria. I told Peter that I planned to escape and asked him to come with me. He said he was scared and didn't want to go with me. He stayed behind and was killed."

I asked Ria what she meant, what she thought happened to Peter. "I'm not exactly sure," she replied, "but I think he ended up in Russia after concentration camp and then came back to Germany. I think he remarried and broke your mother's heart."

I left Poland with the two photos and the thought in my mind that Peter didn't die in the camps as Mutti had always said. If he lived, what happened to him? Why didn't he come to the US with Mutti and my grandparents? Did Mutti know he survived? Or did she assume he died because she never heard from him again? Were they in contact with each other after she came to America? So many questions filled my mind.

Four months later, I found myself in Washington, D.C. for a conference. With two hours free on my last day in DC, I went to the U.S. Holocaust Memorial Museum. I eschewed the familiar exhibits (I had been there several times before) and made a beeline to the research room, which gives visitors access to resources only available at the museum.

As I approached the resource desk, the woman behind the desk was busy talking with someone on the phone. I waited patiently and, when she hung up, said I was there to use the computers to look up family members. She sat me down at the computer behind the desk, even though there were many terminals around the room, so she could help me search.

First, we entered Mutti's name. The screen filled with matching entries. The research assistant clicked on an entry: Mutti's ticket on the U.S.S. Marine Perch, the ship on which she and my grandparents fled Germany to America. She clicked on another entry: Mutti's entire concentration camp record, from the minute she was picked up in Breslau to the moment she was liberated. The research assistant put a ream or more of paper in the printer and hit "Print." All of this was coming home with me.

I glanced at my watch and saw that I didn't have much time before I had to catch my flight. I had left my luggage at my hotel, so I needed to retrieve it on the way to the airport. And it was snowing, which meant it would take longer than usual. But I had the undivided attention of this wonderful research assistant. I had so much more I wanted to search for, but I quickly deduced that I only had time for one more query.

My first instinct was to run a query on my grandmother, Erna Friedlander. But something clicked in my head and instead I said, "Peter Jakobson." I needed to know if Ria was right or wrong. If Mutti had lied. If Peter had survived.

I could hear my heart thumping loudly as the research assistant typed, "Peter Jakobson" into the query line. Nothing. I sighed deeply. Ok, Mutti was right.

Just then, the research assistant interrupted my train of thought, "Wait, let me try another database, the Red

Cross refugee database." I held my breath as she typed in his name again. Within seconds, the screen filled with results.

I had been standing, looking over her shoulder at the computer screen, while she typed in his name. But I instantly sat down when the screen filled with information on Peter. I began to cry and shake. How was this possible?

In went another ream of paper into the printer and I looked at my watch. I really had to leave if I was going to catch my flight. The research assistant clipped both sets of papers and put them in a bag for me to take on the plane. I thanked her and ran back downstairs and out the door to hail a cab.

I barely remember getting to the hotel to pick up my luggage and the subsequent ride to the airport. My flight was delayed, so I sat down for a glass of wine and a bowl of clam chowder while I thumbed through the papers from the Holocaust Museum on Peter. Then, emotionally exhausted from this discovery, I slept the entire flight home.

Once I returned home, I dug into the papers. It became clear that, when Mutti escaped from Ostlinde and left him behind, Peter was captured by the Russians.

He spent five years in a Russian prison camp in Siberia. Without any identification papers, which was the case for every prisoner in a German concentration camp, Peter could not prove that he was a prisoner instead of a Nazi officer, so he was captured and incarcerated.

By the time Peter was released from Siberia, Mutti had been in the United States for five years. She had settled in Aberdeen, Washington with my grandparents and begun a new life. While I can't say for sure what her mental or marital state was at that point, the papers I downloaded at the US Holocaust Memorial Museum clearly show that Peter returned to Germany and contacted my family—my grandfather's sister, Tante Tina—in Darmstadt. In fact, Achim found a photograph of Peter at Tante Tina's house with her sons, Konrad and Paul, at Christmas 1950, in an old box of family photos.

What's more, Red Cross records, which are included in the ream of documents I received from the U.S. Holocaust Memorial Museum, indicate that Peter not only attempted to contact my mother after his release from Siberia, but also applied to emigrate to the United States. The papers clearly read, "Wife emigrated to U.S. in 1946. Wants to join her," and listed Mutti's address in Seattle as of 1950, on Louisa Street.

"What happened to Peter Jakobson?" was now a question to which I needed to find an answer.

YOUR TURN:

- Have you ever spoken with family members about your parent's personality before the Holocaust? Did their personality change or stay the same?

- Have you discovered any wartime secrets kept by your parent or other family members? If so, what were they?

- Have you found any inconsistencies in your parent's Holocaust story, either between different times you spoke with them or between written documents and their verbal stories?

- If you discovered any inconsistencies or secrets, did you proactively follow-up to find the truth? If so, what were the results of your research? Did your findings make you feel happy, sad, or indifferent?

- How did your discoveries change your perception of your parent?

CHAPTER TEN

Mutti's Story

(Note: This chapter is a combination of a transcript I made of one of Mutti's talks to high school students in 1988, her interview with the USC Shoah Foundation, and my own recollections from the countless discussions we had about her experiences)

"Your grandfather's hair turned white overnight, when the Nazis picked up your grandmother for concentration camp."

This is how Mutti began the story every time I asked questions about the Holocaust. The imagery is so strong, even now. I never knew my grandfather (Opi) with anything other than a full head of wavy white hair—which I loved to brush when I was a little girl—but I have seen pictures of him before the Holocaust with a dark or slightly salt-and-pepper mane. Whether or not his hair lost its color in the span of 24 hours, I cannot say for sure, but it's certainly a striking visual to begin a story of enslavement, survival, escape, and reunion.

My grandparents' and Mutti's pre-Holocaust life was spent in Breslau, Germany, which is now known as Wroclaw, Poland. At the time, it boasted one of the largest Jewish populations in Germany and was the second-largest city in East Germany after Berlin. Opi worked at a fabric wholesaler in the Wertheim department store (now Renoma), while Omi washed and folded laundry at the hospital. Mutti attended a Christian school. Summers were filled with visits to Omi's relatives in Beuthen (Bytom) and Opi's relatives in Oppeln (Opole).

My family's apartment on Tauentzienstraße (now Tadeusza Kosciuszki) was near the center of town and very close to both the synagogue and Opi's place of work. Mutti told me that she walked past the synagogue on the way to school, and later work, every day. She never failed to recall how she stopped to watch the synagogue burning on the morning after Kristallnacht.

Omi and Mutti around 1932

The last two years Mutti was in school (1934-1936), she did not get the grades she earned or deserved because she was Jewish. In 1936, her mother (Omi) went to see the principal to see if she should move Mutti to another school where she would be treated more fairly. She was in the 10th grade at the time. The principal told Omi to leave Mutti there, unless he heard something derogatory about her. Her last year, Mutti was the only Jew at the Christian school. She graduated, but not with the high grades she should have received.

Mutti always dreamed of being a foreign correspondent, and she always enjoyed languages (Interestingly, and quite coincidentally, that was my initial career choice as well). She took English in school for six years and French for four years. But, because Hitler forbade Jews from holding jobs of high regard, Mutti's dream was crushed.

Instead, she was given three choices for a career: millinery, beauty salon, or dressmaking. She chose dressmaking (even when she was very young, she would design her own patterns and make her own clothes, using fabric that Opi brought home from work) and started an apprenticeship in 1938.

On November 9th, 1938, Kristallnacht, the world changed forever. All the Jewish men were picked up by the Gestapo and sent to Buchenwald concentration camp, the synagogues burned, Jewish stores were destroyed, and the merchandise from those stores was on the street. Because the Gestapo had files on all the Jews in every town, they could easily pick up whomever they wanted.

My Opi did not get picked up, for two reasons: One, he was born Catholic and converted to Judaism to marry Omi. At that time, the Nazis didn't consider him Jewish. Two, Opi was a WWI veteran and was classified as 50 percent disabled due to a war injury: an exploding grenade sent shrapnel lodging deep in his right elbow, causing massive damage. The doctors who treated him gave him two options for his arm: he could have it set completely straight or he could have it bent at a 90-degree angle. He opted for the latter.

One of my grandparents' friends, a very well-known architect, was picked up that night. Omi and Opi were having dinner at his house with his wife the night he returned from Buchenwald a month later, head shaven and extremely weak. In the time he was gone, his wife had received an affidavit to emigrate to England, however, it was too late: the architect died the same night.

In the fall of 1939, restrictions increased. Hitler declared that every Jew needed to carry an ID card. All females had the name Sarah added as their middle name, all the males, Israel. Also, every Jew had to wear a yellow, fabric Jewish Star of David, pinned to his or her clothes, chest-high. If you were wearing a coat, you had to wear one on your undergarment and another on the coat.

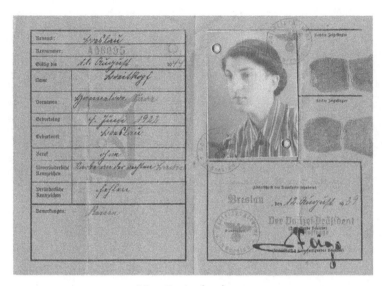

Mutti's Judenkarte

Jews were also issued new ration stamps that had a large "J" printed on them. Not only were rations for Jews much lower than for other individuals, Jews could only shop at designated stores and during specific hours. Jews were only allowed to walk on one particular side of the street, and they could not go to the theatre, watch a movie, or ride on the streetcar or bus. All Jews needed to adhere to a strict curfew.

Eventually, the Nazis rounded up all the Jews in one area of Breslau. My family could stay in their apartment, because the complex was in the designated area. They lived on the fourth floor of the complex, which had retail establishments on the ground floor, including a photo store and a pharmacy.

Good friends of my grandparents, who were Communists, lived on the same floor. Because Jews' consumption of gas, electricity, and water use was severely restricted (they were allowed barely enough electricity to boil water), my Opi figured out how to tap into the electric wires leading to their apartment, so Omi could at least cook. My family paid them back for their usage.

Next, Hitler ordered Jews to turn in all their gold and silver jewelry, flatware, radios, and furs to the Gestapo. On the following holiday, Hitler said Goebbels and Goering were generously giving these items to the German people—and they gave away the Jews' valuables.

Mutti married Peter Jakobson in December 1943 and he moved into my family's apartment. But that "honeymoon" was short-lived, as Mutti and Peter were sent to ZAL (Zwangsarbeitslager or forced labor camp) Schmiegrode in January 1944. The camp was not far from Breslau. Men and women were housed in separate quarters, but they all slept on straw in horse stables. One day in August (August 9th, 1944), Mutti and Peter got wind that their parents would be arriving at the same camp the next morning. They were overjoyed and began to make arrangements to see their parents. However, the Nazis foresaw this scenario, and sent Mutti and Peter—along with other prisoners—to another camp, KZ (Konzentrationslager, or concentration camp) Ostlinde, that night, so they couldn't see their parents.

It turned out that it was only Omi who was sent to Schmiegrode, but she didn't stay there long. Soon after she arrived at the camp, Omi broke her arm and she was sent back home, however, she had to check in with the Gestapo every day. Because of Opi's disability, he was not useful to the Nazis in concentration camp, so they sent him into the center of Breslau cleaning and sweeping streetcars.

In Schmiegrode, Mutti had to dig graves for other prisoners who had died and trenches that would be used for tanks and soldiers in the winter. At Ostlinde, in addition to digging trenches, she cut down trees, and then cut the branches off the trees. The prisoners put the stump across two horses and tied branches around the stump with string. The stumps and branches were then put into the trenches so the trenches wouldn't collapse in the winter rain and snow. All of this work was done wearing only the ubiquitous "striped pajamas," the prison jumpsuit—with the yellow Jewish star—and wooden shoes. Mutti would recall how they would walk in the snow carrying heavy axes. The snow would build up on the soles of the shoes, sometimes as much as six inches, and she and the other prisoners would have to stop and knock off the snow to avoid twisting or rolling their ankles. Escape was practically impossible, with one guard for every five prisoners.

Food in the concentration camp was scarce. Prisoners were fed hot soup—the Nazis called it potato soup, but there were no potatoes in it. Sometimes, they were given a slice of bread when they arrived back at camp after a long day digging graves and trenches and cutting down trees. To survive, Mutti and other prisoners scavenged for other things in the woods, such as beets, to supplement the rations.

Sometime in the winter, Mutti began to complain that she was sick, but the Nazis didn't listen—until one day, she collapsed. The Nazis brought her to a field infirmary and discovered that she had diphtheria, which is highly contagious. So, they shipped her to a hospital near the concentration camp, where she was quarantined, not only because of the diphtheria, but also because she was Jewish.

While she was in the hospital, there were daily air raids, and one day, Mutti heard a funny noise. She stood up on her bed and looked out the window, which was up high for some reason. She saw people walking with wheelbarrows and small carriages piled high with their belongings. She had no idea what was going on.

Later that day, the nurses came through the infirmary and told everyone to get out of the hospital. The ambulatory patients were told to walk, the rest were taken back to the camp via ambulance.

[At this point, I think the story is better told by Mutti herself:]

When the nurse came to me, I asked her where I was going to be sent. The nurse told me, "You're going back to camp." I didn't say anything out loud, but there was no way I was going back to concentration camp.

I waited until darkness fell, but the moon was full or nearly full, so my hospital room and the hallway were illuminated. As I walked into the hallway, my foot hit something: a pile of clothing. Why it was there or whose it was, I didn't know, but I didn't care. I picked up the clothes—a pair of pants, a jacket, and a sweater. Looking around and seeing no one nearby, I slipped into a closet and changed into the clothes, leaving my striped jumpsuit there. I walked out of the hospital and started to walk in the same direction as the crowd of people. They were all walking—or running—west, into the Reich, trying to evade the Russians who were approaching from the east. The scene was utter chaos.

I made it to the railroad station—I didn't have any money, I didn't have anything. But there was no one there to take my money or give out tickets; everyone was just trying to leave because the Russians were approaching.

I turned and asked someone else in the station if there was a train to Breslau arriving anytime soon, and he said, "No, one just left." I decided to just sit down and wait to see what happens.

After a few minutes, a train arrived with wounded soldiers and other private citizens. I asked the conductor where the train was heading and he replied that they were trying to reach Breslau. So, I got on the train.

It was very crowded. We were standing like sardines because everyone wanted on this train and to go west. I slowly made my way to the back of the train car, away from the doors. Pretty soon, I heard a loud voice: "Heil

Hitler! IDs! Heil Hitler!" Well, I didn't have any ID. I didn't know what to do.

While I was standing there (it was dark, of course, because it was the middle of the night), I put my hands behind me and felt something. A doorknob. In Germany, doors open to the inside. I slowly turned the knob and slipped backward into the small room, which contained just a toilet.

I locked the door. The booming voice was coming closer: "IDs! Heil Hitler! IDs!" Finally, soldiers reached the door. They tried to open it, but it wouldn't open. So, they tried to kick it in. It still didn't open. I could hear them talking among themselves and one of them said, "This train probably went through an air raid and the hinges got warped, so the door is stuck." They moved on. I finally breathed.

When the train was about five or six miles outside of Breslau, it stopped. There was an air raid. I made my way to one of the doors and jumped out. I immediately knew where I was; we had stopped where the airport used to be (it had been demolished by the Germans and Russians) and near the Jewish cemetery—at the northern edge of town. I used to go to the cemetery often with my mother, so I knew it well.

I made my way into Breslau, stopping several times for air raids. I didn't go to the main railroad station, because I figured the Gestapo would be there with photos, waiting for people to come back so they could send them back to camp. Later, I found out my hunch was right.

I made my way to my street, Tauenzienstraße, and to our apartment building. I couldn't get in, because the doors were locked. I found out later that both my mother and my father were already there.

I walked over to the telephone booth kitty-corner from our apartment building and checked if there was any money in the change drawer, because sometimes people used the phone and walked away, leaving the change in the compartment. I was lucky: there was.

We had another friend who lived in the front of the apartment complex, and she was also a Communist. I called her.

"I'm back," I said, when she answered.

"I didn't expect you," she replied.

"I know."

"Just come over and I'll let you in."

I walked across the street and she let me in. I immediately went upstairs to the apartment I shared with my parents. They were already there.

Unfortunately, someone must have squealed on us, because the Gestapo appeared the next morning and told us we had to go out and build barricades with the Germany Army to prevent the Russians from entering and conquering Breslau.

A couple of days later after I returned from camp, the entire town was made into a military fortress (Festung), which meant nobody in, nobody out. *[Note: the Siege of Breslau was a three-month stand from February 13th, 1945 to May 6th, 1945]*

Because the airport had been captured by the Russians, the Germans needed to make a new airfield so their planes could land. To do that, they bombed their own citizens' houses and a few churches.

We had to move into the basement of our apartment complex because the Russians were flying small, low-flying aircraft that would shoot into the buildings. On the fourth floor, we were exposed. So we moved to the basement and, as the Russians came closer, the Germans wanted to move into where we were living, so we had to move again.

My father's company was located in a big complex that was somewhat like a galleria, with a courtyard in the center and the wholesale businesses on several floors circling the courtyard. We moved in there. We left everything we had remaining in the basement, and that disappeared once the Germans moved into our building.

We could only go shopping in the morning, because the air raids didn't really begin until later in the day, and we could only shop at specific stores.

A group of Italian soldiers who had fought against Germany—and against Mussolini—were also living in the complex. They had been captured by the Nazis. You would call them POWs.

The Italian soldiers were working for one of the companies that made uniforms for the German army. And since I was a seamstress, they got me to work there too. My job was to sew on buttons, because we didn't have zippers at the time (or they were very rare). When no one was watching, I would cut off the buttons that I had just sewed on, because I didn't want to help the Nazis.

To get to work, I had to walk in a tunnel that ran under the courtyard. One morning, I hit my head on something. I looked up: There were three bombs. We knew something had happened during the night, because the building shook, but we didn't know what. We thought the Russians had bombed us.

I went back home and called the bomb squad. When they arrived, they opened the bombs and found that each one had the same note inside: "This is all we can do for you." *[Note: I always assumed there was also some food or other humanitarian aid, but Mutti never mentioned it]* We don't know who actually dropped the fake bombs, it could have been some Russians or some Germans, but we know we were very lucky that day.

I worked at the uniform factory from February to May of 1945. On the 8th of May, the Russians entered Breslau. Breslau actually surrendered after Berlin.

Everyone who wanted to leave Breslau had to walk, because the railroads were destroyed. Most people left with their belongings in a wheelbarrow and began walking toward West Germany. If you look at a map, you can see that it's quite a long distance between Breslau and the border. *[Note: the border no longer exists, as Germany is now reunified]*

Most of the Russian officers were Jewish because they spoke Yiddish, which is a mixture of Russian, Polish, and German. One day, we heard a lot of commotion and noise outside, and my mother went upstairs to see what was going on. She wouldn't let me go upstairs, because it was too dangerous.

When she looked outside, she saw Russian soldiers looting everywhere. They had never seen watches, or bicycles, or even flush toilets. Then she saw a short Russian officer walking with his adjutant. The adjutant blew his whistle and the other soldiers stopped looting and stood at attention in front of the short officer. My mother figured that he must be a high-ranking officer to command this authority, so she went up to him and spoke to him in German.

"I am Jewish," she told him.

He looked at her and responded in Yiddish, "Mother, you're Jewish?"

She said, "Yes."

The officer turned to his adjutant and said in Russian, "Hold everything here, I want to talk with this woman."

He then asked her if she had any children, and she replied that yes, she had a daughter.

The officer said, "Let me see her."

My mother, worried, asked, "Will you promise not to do anything to her?"

He replied, "Yes, I promise. I am Jewish too and I will not hurt her."

So, my mother came downstairs with the officer, to where I was sitting with my father—in the basement.

He asked me if I spoke Yiddish or Hebrew. I decided to answer by reciting the Shema [Note: the Shema is the most famous Jewish prayer that begins, "Hear O Israel, the Lord is our G-d, the Lord is One." At that moment, the Russian officer believed we were Jewish.

He then asked us what we had to eat. We didn't have much; I think we had one loaf of bread left and a little meat.

He handed each of us a pass and said, "Tomorrow is Friday and it's Shabbat. I would like you to come to my place for Shabbat dinner."

The next evening, we set out to go to the Russian officer's house for dinner. We had to go to the other side of town, but all we had to do was show the pass to officers on the way and they let us pass.

When we arrived, the Russian officer was seated behind a big desk and he was smoking a big cigar. He was writing something, but when we walked in, he stopped and asked us, "Do you know what I'm doing? Today is Shabbat and I'm writing to my mother that I just met the first Jews in Germany." He was from Kiev.

He then sent his adjutant to get food for us. He brought so much that they had to send two other officers with us to carry it home. But before we left, the Russian officer looked at my parents and said, "You can use the pass I gave you to get around," but when he looked at me, he said, "There's nothing I can do to help you. Even the pass won't protect you."

The Russian soldiers would rape at any time, and just because I had a pass, it wouldn't prevent them from raping me if they wanted to. Once, we heard a loud scream in the basement apartment next to ours, and then we heard a shot. We found out later that a Russian soldier had raped the wife and the husband tried to stop him. The soldier just turned around and shot the husband dead.

I was almost caught by the Russians twice. Every night, the Italians, one of whom was named Roberto and was from Turin, along with a group of Belgians would hold a séance to ask the spirits what the next day would bring. I was there with them one night when they held this séance and they threw me out, because I said I didn't believe in it. They told me not to come to their séances again because the ghosts wouldn't answer them when I was there.

Roberto had asked me to get his uniform in order, so he could wear it when the Russians came. And one day, when all three of us (my mother, my father, and I) were in their basement apartment having dinner, there was a knock on the door.

We opened the door and saw two Russian officers, both women, standing there. We were eating spaghetti, and I could hardly eat.

I remember exactly how we were seated. The two Russian officers were across the round table from me on the left. The three Italians were seated directly across from me and to the right. The Belgians were seated to my right. Then it was my mother, father, and I, and then Roberto to our left.

The officers started pointing at each of us and asking, "You! Italian?" "Yes." "You, Italian?" "Yes." Shortly before the Russian officers got to my mother, father, and I, Roberto interjected in Russian, "I told you, we are all Italian!" The Russians inexplicably turned around and left without a word.

The second time I was almost caught, I was alone in our apartment, about to get dressed. I heard the Russians approaching and looked for a place to hide. I knew they would find me easily in our apartment, so I couldn't stay there. There was a hospital in our complex (all the hospitals had to be underground because of bombing) and I decided to run all the way to the back of the hospital. I found some bunk beds and jumped into one of them, covering myself up to my neck, because I wasn't dressed. A soldier came through and lifted all the bed-covers. I don't know why, but shortly before he got to me, he stopped and turned around.

Soon after that, the Russians ordered all foreigners to wear their country's colors. The Jewish colors are blue and white. I went to the factory, found some blue and white ribbon, and made small pins for my parents and myself.

One night, the entire center of town was in flames. On moonlit nights, the Russians could see where to drop their bombs, but if it was cloudy or a new moon, they would set flares that we called "Christmas Trees" that would illuminate the town so they could see where to bomb. That night, they had set Christmas Trees everywhere.

We finally found a new place to stay, about 10 or 15 minutes from Wertheim, and we moved out of the basement apartment. My mother and I had little purses that I had made and we each had a watch. My mother had my birth certificate and our affidavit to come to the U.S. in her purse. We had received the affidavit in 1938, but 10 quota numbers before ours, the war broke out.

As we walked from the basement to the new apartment, we ran into some Russian soldiers. They asked us what time it was. Because Russian is close to Polish, although it's written in a different alphabet, my father understood the question. He looked at his watch and the Russian took it.

Another time my father walked from our new apartment to the old one in the basement at Wertheim, the Russians stopped him and took all his clothes. He came home in his underwear.

In September of 1945, we left Breslau on buses paid for by the Jewish Committee. Just before we left, some of us were called together because one of the men who sent us to concentration camp approached one of the Jewish leaders and asked him to save his life because he claimed that he didn't do anything to us. Our leader said, "You did enough. You sent us all to concentration camp. I'm not going to save you." And then, he called the Russian Polizia.

The man ran away, but we all got together to try to find him—and we did. He was hiding under a big pile of coal. We called the Russian Polizia, and as far as I know they shot him.

We left Breslau that day on those buses. But whatever we had acquired between the time we were liberated from concentration camp and when we left Breslau, the Russians took away from us.

We had to be very careful on our journey, because the streets still contained hidden landmines. We lived in Erfurt for a year, until the end of May 1946. I worked for the Jewish Committee in Erfurt.

We left Erfurt in May 1946 with another Jewish transport, in cattle cars. We wanted to get to Frankfurt, where the American Consulate was. We had to cross the border *[Note: Erfurt was in East Germany and Frankfurt was in West Germany]* but the border that would take us directly across was closed. So instead, we went up to Hannover. We arrived on my birthday *[Note: June 4ᵗʰ]* and that's the first time we had tea and cookies since before the war. We stayed overnight at the Jewish Committee and traveled to Frankfurt the next day, where we had arranged to stay with friends in nearby Wiesbaden.

The next day, I set out for the American consulate. My parents were physically ok after everything we had endured but mentally, they were not too well, so I went alone. I walked the 25 or so miles from Wiesbaden to the American Consulate in Frankfurt.

At the consulate, the man asked a slew of questions: "Are all three of you Jewish?" "Were you all in concentration camp?" "Did you ever have any intention to go to America?" I could answer all three questions yes and I had proof.

I wanted to make the first ship out of Germany, but we missed it, so we got on the second ship. Before we could board the ship, we had to go through a DP (displaced persons) camp. There, I saw people I knew, but many of them had gray hair now, even though they didn't just a few months ago. I thought, "That's funny, they weren't gray when I saw them last." I couldn't figure it out but then I realized that they had white powder on their heads so they wouldn't get lice. And that's how I found out why everyone had white hair.

We left Bremen on the USS Marine Perch on the 22nd of August and arrived in NY on the 31st of August, which was a Saturday, just before Labor Day. Everyone was on deck as we approached New York, and I don't think you will ever have the same feeling as we did when we saw the Statue of Liberty: Free. To come to a free country, you don't know what it means. Nobody asks you questions, nobody asks if you are Jewish or what your religion is? It's just something that you cannot imagine. My mother's brother, my Onkel Fritz, had sent money to us in New

York. He couldn't come himself because he had business to attend to in Aberdeen, Washington, where he lived.

We stayed in New York for two or three days before taking the train to Aberdeen, where we lived for the next three years with my Onkel Fritz and his English Springer Spaniel, Beau. Since I was a seamstress, I started working the following week at Wolf's Department Store in the alterations department.

In late 1949 or early 1950, my parents and I moved to Seattle, where my father and I both worked at Boeing Corporation. My mother worked at Swedish Hospital in the laundry department.

I met Fred Wanderer in July 1963 at a Fourth of July picnic in Seattle. Fred and I were married on September 1st, 1963, and I moved to Portland, where Fred had a lumber wholesaling business, Fred Wanderer Lumber Company. My daughter, Emily, was born in November 1964.

YOUR TURN:

- Was/were your parent/parents open about his/her/their Holocaust experiences?

- What do you know about their history? Do you have a video recording, audio recording, written history, and/or other supporting data?

- Have you sat down with your parent/parents/grandparents and interviewed them yourself? If not, can you do that now? Did you create a questionnaire to help guide the interview?

- Have you created or attempted to create a timeline of events for your parent's/parents' Holocaust experience? If not, spend some time doing that now. Get one or two large pieces of paper and tape them to a wall. Put down as many milestones on the timeline as you know.

CONCLUSION

I spent the majority of my childhood hiding the fact that Mutti was a Holocaust survivor. Desperate to fit in and not be "different," it was hard enough to be Jewish in a mainly Christian suburb of Portland, with older parents (Mutti was 42 and Vati was 56 when I was born), and—the horror!—older parents with foreign (German) accents. I was tired of having the specter of the Holocaust hanging over everything I said and did. I was angry that I couldn't be a normal kid with 'normal' parents. Every day I felt re-traumatized, because each day, the Holocaust managed to make an appearance somehow, thanks to Mutti.

In fact, my freshman year at Cal, I wanted nothing to do with Judaism at all. I didn't tell people I was Jewish (Wanderer isn't a recognizably Jewish name). I didn't go to Hillel. I avoided the Chabad house (literally, I would walk on the other side of the street). I didn't observe the High Holidays or Passover. For the first time in my life, I actually felt free of daily judgment and living in the past. I could finally move on and look forward to the future. I could finally breathe.

I don't think I had volunteered the final detail about Mutti to anyone until my sophomore year in college. I remember being surprised at the reaction of my sorority sister when I told her: she was fascinated. I had expected, even assumed, a negative reaction or worse, indifference. I don't even know why. Perhaps it was a fear of anti-Semitism. She asked me a few questions about Mutti and I slowly pieced together the story that I had heard Mutti tell so many times in the past. Her jaw dropped and she wanted to know more. I started to realize that people wanted to know Mutti's story, to understand her bravery, and I began to tell her story more freely. But no one asked how her trauma affected me, and I didn't connect the dots either. It was just something that happened to Mutti that I had to deal with, I thought.

Does my experience resonate with you? Did you hide your family's Holocaust history because you didn't know how others would react or because you were fearful of opening a Pandora's box of emotions? Did you have a conflicted relationship with Judaism, either rejecting it for a while or perhaps, did you come to know about your Jewishness (and/or your Holocaust history) later in life and now want to have a stronger connection with Judaism? Whatever your story, you can work through much of the residue of the Holocaust by writing—and sharing your stories with the world—as I have done.

The anger I had about the constant mentions of Hitler, Germany, and how her life was ruined by the Holocaust didn't dissipate until after I started writing, two months after Mutti's death in December of 2014. For years, I had covered my eyes and ears at any mention of the Holocaust. Then I began to accept it and speak about it freely, embracing the 2G label. Finally, after drawing the lines between her experiences and mine, I stopped blaming Mutti for physically and emotionally abusing me, and I started to delve deep into how and why she treated me the way she did.

Through writing, I was able to find the compassion for Mutti and understand that she did the best she could, because of her Holocaust trauma. And only then did I realize how broken I was. I was unhappy—miserable, really. I loved my kids but I hated my life. I felt trapped in a life that was what Mutti wanted for me, not what I wanted for myself. I was not the best mother I could be. I was not the best wife I could be. I wasn't the authentic me at all.

The more I wrote, the more I saw that I *needed* to write this. In order to heal myself, and heal my children, I needed to go through this process of introspection and accept myself. I moved back to Portland, my hometown, where I have a huge support network that I never had in California.

In the process of writing, it also became abundantly clear to me—and to many others with whom I discussed the general topic—that the transference of trauma by the actual victims to their progeny is not limited to those who survived the Holocaust. Many of the connections I drew between Mutti's experiences and my personality, behavior, and choices could likely be drawn between victims of other genocides (e.g., Bosnia, Rwanda, Darfur, Iraq, and most recently, Syria) and their children and grandchildren, as well as between victims of other types of trauma (e.g., the Jonestown and Branch Davidian cults) and their offspring as well.

Exploring trauma through writing and storytelling is something I've been able to help many others cope with and I've witnessed incredible results. Most of my clients claim they are less angry and resentful after writing their stories, and they now have a positive outlook on life. Some are taking more risks than ever before and have told me that, after writing about and releasing their trauma, they are truly living life for the first time. And several clients discovered the underlying sources of trauma that they didn't know existed through writing.

My wish is that, after reading my story, you realize that you're not alone in your struggle. You don't need to suffer in silence. You can begin to release your second-hand trauma through writing and, after working with the writing prompts at the end of each chapter, you can see how powerful and transformative storytelling can be.

Ode to a Fly Swatter

I have no idea what happened to that green fly swatter with the gray handle. I'm guessing Mutti threw it away, as she did so many things of value and not, when she moved from Portland to Seattle. I don't remember ever seeing it in her different apartments in Seattle. Maybe it was her way of leaving the past behind too.

But it doesn't have to be a green fly swatter with a gray handle to evoke my feelings of fear and shame. Any fly swatter will do.

Someone gave me a fly swatter once—an odd gift, for sure, but clearly not a welcome one for me. It's yellow with a really long white handle and a red loop of yarn at the end from which to hang it. The yellow swatter head has a deceivingly beautiful flower pattern. It hangs in the closet with the cleaning supplies. I've never used it. In fact, I've never used a fly swatter at all. And I suspect I never will.

Acknowledgments

I want to thank Amy for pushing me to start writing in the first place, two months after Mutti died. And Verda, my first writing coach, who encouraged me to put myself in the story and helped me get in touch with emotions that I didn't even know I had.

Many thanks also go to Lisa Romeo, writer extraordinaire, who reviewed my first attempts at writing my stories (before I knew I had a book) and turned most of them on their heads with fantastic edits and suggestions, making them so much better.

Much of this journey would not have taken place if not for Michlean Amir at the research desk at the U.S. Holocaust Memorial Museum in Washington, D.C., who checked that "one last database" before I caught my flight back to the Bay Area.

My favorite cousin, Achim. You helped Mutti in so many ways when she was alive, and I know she was immensely grateful. I never would have found Peter's family in Germany without your generous and tireless work. Danke vielmals.

What can I say about my PDX Jew Crew? Felicia, Sallie, Debbie, Stacy, Dan, Glenn, and Mark, your warm welcome back to Portland will never be forgotten. Friends for life, indeed. And a special shout-out to my "big brother," Bob: you will always be my favorite shrink. Thanks for not charging me because I'd be flat broke by now!

Brad: from the VW bus taking us to Hillel Academy to the NYC subway, your friendship and support means the world to me. Thank you for always being there.

Thank you, Carolyn, for FaceTiming me when you sense I need to talk and for being my sports BFF. There's no one I'd rather talk about tennis, baseball, basketball, or football with than you. Well, there's no one else who WOULD talk tennis with me at 4:00AM during the Aussie Open. And thank you for not finding and posting the photo of me in the baby blue velour pantsuit.

The Aloha High School gang—Lisa, Jeanne, Dalibor, Mike, Bill, Trent, Mielle, and Maura—your words of encouragement and faith kept me writing forward. RIP Trent, I hope you're making MacDaddys in heaven.

Debbie, Claire, and Michelle, you gals make Loyally in Epsilon Pi really mean something.

Thank you, Tanya and Dell. You know why you're here. Namaste.

To Kristin, my BFF. You got me through the lowest of lows and spent hours on the phone talking and texting. I truly could not have made it to the other side without you.

To Judy and Al, who were always there for me when Mutti and I had one of our epic fights. No words can adequately express my gratitude for all those nights in high school when I sought refuge on Dover Street. And perhaps even more importantly, thank you for graciously letting me stay at your house in Seaside for my final push to complete this book.

Sharon, thanks for getting me to see that love is the drug I was looking for and for introducing me to Angela and The Author Incubator.

And to Angela Lauria, who had the vision that this could be more than a simple catharsis book and showed me that I could truly help others work through their trauma, as well. Megan Jo, my sister from the other Portland:

you changed my world with one simple comment on a Saturday evening in Virginia. Thank you! And thanks to my entire Idea to Done cohort—you all rock!

To the Morgan James Publishing team: Special thanks to David Hancock, CEO & Founder for believing in me and my message. To my Author Relations Manager, Margo Toulouse, thanks for making the process seamless and easy. Many more thanks to everyone else, but especially Jim Howard, Bethany Marshall, and Nickcole Watkins.

About the Author

Emily Wanderer Cohen is the daughter and granddaughter of Holocaust survivors. Ever since the day she came home from religious school asking her mother about the Holocaust, Emily heard her mother's stories of incarceration in and es-cape from concentration camp as well as eventual immigration to the United States. Her mother also spoke to schoolchildren and other audiences about her personal Holocaust experiences, helping to ensure that this horrific event would never be forgotten. Emily now works with multiple generations of Holocaust survivors to understand their transmitted trauma and heal it through writing. She also speaks to Jewish and other organizations about her mother's history as well as how her mother's trauma affected her as a second-generation (2G) Holocaust survivor.

Website: www.fromgentogenbook.com

Facebook: https://www.facebook.com/coachemilycohen

Twitter: @emilygcohen

THANK YOU

Thank you so much for sharing my journey. The fact that you've gotten to this point in the book tells me something important about you: you're ready to shift out of circling around your transmitted trauma and begin a new path to the future. You're ready to bring hope and peace into your days.

Most importantly, you're ready to free your mind of the old stories and the things you can't control. Don't think of this as the end of a book; think about it as the beginning of a transformative, life-changing journey to healing your intergenerational trauma.

To help you gain clarity about which trauma triggers covered in this book (and others that aren't covered) may be affecting you, I've created **The Intergenerational Trauma Quiz.** It's a simple diagnostic tool to help you discover where you may want to focus your initial healing efforts.

To access the assessment, simply go to www.from-gentogenbook.com/bonus

Morgan James
Speakers Group

➤ www.TheMorganJamesSpeakersGroup.com

We connect Morgan James published
authors with live and online events
and audiences who will benefit
from their expertise.

Morgan James makes all of our titles available through the Library for All Charity Organization.

www.LibraryForAll.org

Printed in the USA
CPSIA information can be obtained
at www.ICGtesting.com
JSHW021416160824
R13664500001B/R136645PG68134JSX00023B45